MAKING
CARDS
WITH
RUBBER
STAMPS

**OVER 100 ILLUSTRATED
PROJECTS AND
INSPIRATIONAL IDEAS**

Maggie Wright

David & Charles

To a best friend, an incredible father to my children and a husband who is my total inspiration. Derek, this is for you.

A DAVID & CHARLES BOOK

First published in the UK in 2003
Reprinted 2003, 2004

Copyright © Maggie Wright 2003

Distributed in North America
by F&W Publications, Inc.
4700 East Galbraith Road
Cincinnati, OH 45236
1-800-289-0963

Maggie Wright has asserted her right to be identified as author of this work in accordance with the Copyright, Designs and Patents Act, 1988.

A catalogue record for this book is available from the British Library.

ISBN 0 7153 1528 5 hardback
ISBN 0 7153 1529 3 paperback (USA only)

Printed in Italy by Rotolito Lombarda SpA
for David & Charles
Brunel House   Newton Abbot   Devon

Commissioning Editor Fiona Eaton
Desk Editor Jennifer Proverbs
Executive Art Editor Ali Myer
Designer Nigel Morgan
Production Controller Jennifer Campbell

Visit our website at www.davidandcharles.co.uk

David & Charles books are available from all good bookshops; alternatively you can contact our Orderline on (0)1626 334555 or write to us at FREEPOST EX2 110, David & Charles Direct, Newton Abbot, TQ12 4ZZ (no stamp required UK mainland).

Contents

Introduction

In the time it takes you to run to the store and select a greetings card, you could create your own unique hand-stamped design. It is that simple. What is more, in this world of hi-tech communication, the individuality and care you invest in your hand-crafted cards will make them especially appreciated and prized by the loved ones and friends who receive them.

The wonders of stamping

If, like me, you struggle to draw, stamping can help to unleash your latent creativity by giving you the confidence to step forward into the world of art. Use stamps as a tool to fulfil the aspirations of the artist in you. Another of the many reasons why stamping is so popular is that it is amazingly therapeutic – it frees up your imagination and allows you to lose yourself in the totally absorbing, exacting and satisfying techniques involved.

The nature of stamps

Learn how to give your cards a professional finish with techniques such as gold embossing (see pages 52–53).

Rubber stamps are, as you would expect, made from rubber and usually mounted on maple blocks. These generally carry a print of the image, which helps with recognition and placement. Foam-mounted stamps, which generally come in sets, are much cheaper to buy. Foam-block home decoration stamps, for use on walls and fabric, are very inexpensive and also work well on card – they feature in the shadow stamping project in the book, on pages 20–21. New on the market are transparent polymer stamps, which can be removed from their acrylic block. These are cheaper than regular rubber stamps and make placement very straightforward. They also enable you to build up several images by placing more than one stamp on a large block.

In today's marketplace, there is a stamp to cover every conceivable occasion and subject. But you do not have to buy every one – one stamp can be used for several themes, or only colour in part of a stamp or use a large stamp on a small card for a strikingly different result. Team up with friends for a monthly stamping session, when you can share and swap stamps. It is a great idea to stamp with friends, giving you the opportunity to brainstorm and come up with totally new concepts.

Stamp care

Stamps should be cleaned every time you use them, to prevent the different ink colours from muddying one other. It also helps to prolong the life of the stamps. Never soak wood stamps in water, as this might loosen the rubber die. Keep stamps away from sunlight when not in use.

There are many different stamp cleaners available. DIY or hardware stores sell paint pads, which work well for cleaning stamps. Draw the stamp one way through the wet pad, then dry on kitchen paper. Alternatively, you can make your own pad out of old towels, one to dampen and one to dry. Always be careful when cleaning that you do not inadvertently spray or drip water onto your work.

How to use this book

This book presents a wide range of creative ideas and projects. Each project introduces and applies a new technique, or builds on a previous technique, to provide the maximum variety of design and finish, and bring new dimensions to your stamping work. In general, projects earlier in the book are the easiest, progressing to the more challenging later on. Your new-found skills will also enable you to create your own, alternative designs, and always bear in mind that most of the projects can be done with any stamp you own – it is the technique that is important. The card galleries at the end of the book are an excellent source of inspiration for all occasions, and feature

Creating this stunning card will provide hours of fun for the whole family (see pages 76–77).

techniques used in the projects. Do not be afraid to experiment and make mistakes – this is the best way to discover new approaches and ideas.

Before you start

Always make sure that your work surface is level, smooth and uncluttered. Have plenty of scrap paper or a drawing pad handy to test a new stamp and check that it stamps evenly – every stamp has its own character. This will prevent you from wasting expensive card.

Get yourself organized before you begin a project. Have your Basic Tool Kit ready (see page 6), then read through the project instructions carefully and assemble the specialist materials and tools in the 'You will need…' list. Work with an old towel on your knees in case you want to wipe your stamp, tools or hands, to save you having to get up. Clean and clear away everything once you have finished the project in preparation for your next stamping session.

Extend your creative skills to making memorable gift tags (see page 80).

Start stamping!

My vision as a stamp artist is to inspire you as others have inspired me. I hope this book succeeds in sparking the inner fire of creativity in you and takes your stamp art to new levels.

So turn off the television, turn on your favourite music and pick up a stamp!

Tools

Some of the tools needed for the projects in this book are items of basic equipment that you probably already have. But you will need a limited range of specialist tools to produce professional-looking results. However, be cautious about investing in a lot of extra kit – you can always add to it once you have progressed in your stamping work to more ambitious designs.

Basic Tool Kit

Many of the following items are used in every project and are therefore not included in the 'You will need…' lists. Assemble these tools together before you begin any project.

scissors

craft knife

ruler

bone folder

cutting mat

paper trimmer

sharp pencil

paintbrushes

double-sided tape

craft glue

spray adhesive

To follow are the tools you will come across in the projects, which are pictured on the facing page.

1 *Rubber stamps* There are two types of stamp design – solid, where there are no areas to colour in, and fine line, providing an outline within which areas can be coloured in. The latter are suitable for embossing; generally speaking, script stamps are the only solid stamps that are embossed.

2 *Heat gun* Use to melt embossing powders when embossing a design – hairdryers are not hot enough. Care must be taken when using a heat gun that the surface onto which you are directing the heat is not painted or lacquered underneath, otherwise the intensity of the heat could cause damage. Work over a clay floor tile to protect your work surface. Keep the tool out of reach of young children when in use and afterwards, in case of residual heat.

3 *Paper trimmer* There are several types available. These make it easy to measure and cut card pieces accurately.

4 *Craft knife* Use to cut out stamped images and masks or to trim card. Always use with a self-healing mat to protect your work surfaces. Protect the blade with a sheath.

5 *Ruler* A transparent ruler aids accurate placement. Use a metal ruler, with a craft knife, for cutting straight edges, as you may nick a plastic ruler with the blade.

6 *Round-nosed pliers and wire cutters* (latter not pictured) These two items are essential if you work with wire or metal. The pliers enable you to bend and shape wire (see page 81). Wire cutters cut not only wire but also metal sheets and wire mesh.

7 *Eraser* There are various specialist erasers, such as for chalk, pencil and crayon removal. There is also an eraser that removes glue, which is very useful.

8 *Eyelet fixing tool and punch, hammer and mat* This collection of tools is the essential kit for applying eyelets to cards, either as an attractive and effective way of holding card pieces together, or to provide neatly finished holes for threading through ribbon and other decorative uses. (See Fixing Eyelets, page 49.)

9 *Brayer* These rollers come in various sizes and are used to spread ink evenly over a surface, working especially well on gloss card. They can cover a large area of card quickly in a graduation of colours (see page 36–37).

10 *Scissors* You will need a good pair of sharp, pointed scissors for cutting paper. Small scissors are useful for cutting more intricate shapes.

11 *Paintbrushes* Various sizes of paintbrush are needed for colouring in images. An aqua brush, filled with water, can be used for watercolour painting projects. A large, dry paintbrush is ideal for dusting off excess embossing powder or brushing away decorating chalk where not required.

12 *Rolling pin* Use for rolling out polymer clay (see page 62) or for flattening shrink plastic after shrinking (see pages 75 and 77).

TIP

To protect your fingers when using a heat gun, hold the card with a clothes peg.

13 *Holepunch* This is a $\frac{1}{16}$in holepunch, or a micro holepunch; other holepunches are available for cutting different-sized holes, such as $\frac{1}{4}$in or $\frac{1}{8}$in, for threading through different thicknesses of wire (see pages 30–31) or ribbon (see page 34–35). Unlike the eyelet holepunch (see item 8), these punches have a limited reach.

14 *Deckle-edged scissors* This is just one of the many types of decorative-edged scissors available; other designs include scallop and postage stamp.

15 *Sponges* Different shapes are available, including round and wedge, for applying and blending inks from either brush markers (see page 40) or ink pads to create a textured-looking background (see pages 26–27) or the impression of sea, sand or grass. A rough sponge is used to rub off excess metal leaf (see pages 60–61).

16 *Punches* These come in many different sizes and designs, from flowers and animals to Christmas borders, photo corners, squares, circles and tags. Special punch aids are available if you find some punches hard to use. Punched-out images look effective mounted with 3-D foam pads, or small shapes grouped together, such as flowers to form a bouquet. Border punches can give a lacy look to the edge of cards. Square punches are a great way of cutting card to layer or collage, or to make frames and tags.

17 *Xyron™ Sticker Machine* This is perfect for applying adhesive to ribbons, punched images, cord and thin strips of vellum.

TIP
To sharpen punches, then keep them sharp over time, carefully punch through kitchen foil a few times

Materials

Every stamper should at least have a black pigment ink pad, but beyond that there is a bewildering array of inks on the market for rubber stamping and it is important to know which type is suitable for which particular technique. Other decorating products also abound, so use the notes below to help guide you through the minefield.

1 *Permanent ink pads* Solvent- or dye-based, and generally without the need for heat-setting, these can be used on a variety of surfaces. Permanent ink images, when dry, can be coloured in using brush markers or watercolour pencils without the stamped image bleeding or muddying. Some permanent inks may be slow drying enough to be embossed. Ancient Page™ is permanent on most surfaces, while Stazon™ works well on wood, glass and fabric.

2 *Pigment ink pads* These are slow drying, enabling you to use them for embossing with clear embossing powder (see pages 26–27). They come in a wide variety of vivid, pastel, earth and metallic colours and in all shapes and sizes such as petal wheels, small squares, cubes and cat's eyes (pictured). All these ink pads will ink a stamp from the smallest to the largest because the foam is raised above its plastic container.

3 *Dye-based ink pads* Water-based, quick drying and available in a stunning range of colours, these can be used for stamping on all papers, but colours may bleed a little on absorbent and uncoated papers; coated gloss paper is ideal. Vivid™ ink pads are really vibrant. The ink takes a long time to dry on vellum but can be successfully embossed with clear embossing powder. Pads come in many sizes, including small cubes, as shown.

TIP

To prevent dye-based inked designs from fading over time, spray with a special lacquer glaze at a distance in a well-ventilated area.

4 *Brilliance™ ink pads* These are water-based pigment inks that are archival (acid-free) and dry to perfection on wood, vellum, polymer clay, gloss card and shrink plastic. They are also great for sponging.

5 *Multicoloured dye-based ink pads* These come in regular and long sizes, and you can choose which range of colours on the pad to ink your stamp with (see page 32).

6 *Resist-ink pads* (not pictured) These are specially formulated to repel water-based dye inks on gloss paper. Resist-inked images must be dried with a heat gun, then you can brayer over them with coloured inks and see them emerge (see pages 36–37). VersaMark™, can also been used to emboss or adhere chalk to the stamped image (see page 46).

TIP

Re-inkers are now available for most ink pads, but keep lids on pads when not in use or when using a heat gun nearby to prevent pads drying out.

7 *Clear embossing ink pad* Slow-drying and colourless or slightly tinted, this ink is designed for use with coloured embossing powder.

8 *Coloured and metallic embossing powders* These powders are sprinkled over wet images stamped with slow-drying ink, then heated to fuse the powder to the ink and in turn to the card (see pages 52 and 54). Coloured powders are opaque and are available in an incredible range of colours. Metallic powders come in different sizes of granulation – fine, regular and thick.

9 *Clear embossing powder* This is used to emboss images stamped with slow-drying coloured ink. Once heated, it allows the colour underneath to shine through.

10 *Gold glitter embossing powder* This is gold embossing powder mixed with gold crystal glitter, to give an extra sparkle to the embossed image (see pages 58–59). A hologram glitter can also be added to clear powder; when heated a range of colours appear, for an interesting effect.

11 *Embossing pens* These contain a slow-drying ink that remains wet long enough to be embossed and can be used for addressing envelopes or drawing your own designs, adding coloured embossing powder and heat embossing. Dual embossing pens have a dual point for colouring in and a chisel point for calligraphy writing. They can be used directly on the rubber, stamped out and clear embossed, or used to colour the stamped image and clear embossed (see pages 56–57).

12 *Glue pens* These are handy for sticking lightweight papers together and for applying loose glitter to particular areas.

13 *Double-sided tape* Ideal for sticking light- to medium-weight papers together. Use spray adhesive for bonding heavier weights of paper.

14 *Liquid Appliqué*™ Applied to areas of a stamped design and then gently heated, this liquid rises to create a fluffy effect (see page 80). If, however, you leave it for 24 hours, then heat, you get a wonderfully smooth finish, which can be painted.

15 *Puff Static Bag* This is used to wipe over cards to prevent embossing powder sticking to unwanted areas. Use sparingly on dark card.

16 *Wax coloured pencils* These are used for colouring in stamped images and shades can be blended together (see pages 22–23). Watercolour pencils are used in the same way but blended with a little water from a paintbrush.

17 *Glitter glue* These come in a dazzling array of colours. They take 20–30 minutes to dry if applied sparingly.

18 *Loose crystal glitter* Again available in a range of colours, this glitter can be applied to card using a glue pen.

19 *Brush markers* These water-based brush pens, available in different colours and with different-sized tips (see pages 16–17), can be applied directly to the stamp rubber or used to colour in stamped images. You can use them for watercolouring by blending the colours onto a palette and applying with a wet paintbrush.

20 *Liquid Pearls*™ These dispense droplets of different pearlized colours to highlight details of a stamped image, such as flower centres (see page 33).

21 *Dimensional Magic*™ This highlights and adds clear dimension to areas of a design (see page 23). Allow up to three hours to dry.

22 *Decorating chalks* These are great for colouring in stamped designs or creating decorative backgrounds (see pages 44–45 and 50–51) and give a soft, pastel effect. They can also be used with a VersaMark™ resist-ink pad to adhere the chalk (see pages 46–47).

Papers & Card

Papers, papers everywhere! There has never been such an abundance of decorative papers and card. All kinds of intriguing specialist papers made the world over are now easily available. These can be used in many different creative ways in conjunction with rubber stamping to produce truly unique card designs.

There is also a tremendous variety in card in terms of colour, size, shape, weight and finish. You will need a fairly heavy weight of card if you are sending the finished card by itself or if you are using it as a base card and layering onto it. Card used for layering can be of a lesser weight, as the strength will come from the base card.

Papers

Handmade papers These come in a variety of textures and weights. They can be expensive but often come in large sheets that could be shared among your fellow stampers. Some have threads, flower petals or leaves embedded, which provide added textural interest as well as subtle, natural colours and pattern.

Exotic papers This group of papers includes Oriental-style paper, including Chinese character paper, and Egyptian hieroglyphic paper. Mulberry paper from Thailand, with its fibrous swirls, remains a firm favourite among stamping enthusiasts.

Background papers The diversity of design and colour of these papers has become totally mind-blowing since the art of scrapbooking took off – there is one to suit whatever stamp project you have in mind. Background papers come in A4 or US letter sizes and 30.5cm (12in) squares. So again, cut in half and share with a friend.

Vellum papers These papers are fast becoming a favourite with stampers and are available in a wonderful range of shades, patterns and embossed textures. They can be used to create arty backdrops by roughly tearing to shape. A soft effect can be achieved by stamping and then colouring the image on the reverse side (see pages 83 and 85).

Velvet or suede papers These add a touch of luxury to any stamped image, especially if gold glitter embossing powder is used (see pages 58–59).

Other papers Wallpapers, giftwrap, tissue paper and even napkins can create reasonably priced backgrounds or can be stamped on. They are also ideal to use for collage designs.

Card

Matt and linen finishes These are great for embossing or regular stamping with ink pads. The linen will give a subtle, handmade look.

Gloss finish This is perfect for using with dye-based inks, giving a vibrant and professional finish.

Pearlized card This makes a lovely soft backdrop on which to stamp.

Watercolour card This is the best for all watercolour projects, as it is not inclined to buckle when wet.

Shaped cards There are many shaped card blanks available which you can select to tie in with a particular occasion, such as a Christmas tree for Christmas (see page 76), gloves for a wedding and a heart for a Valentine's card.

TIP
Never throw away any pieces of scrap paper or card – even the smallest piece could be stamped, punched or used in another decorative way.

Embellishments

Embellishments enhance any stamped card and allow you to express your own individuality in your designs. There is a treasure trove of decorative bits and pieces out there waiting for you to exploit in this way. Incredible fun can be had just by collecting together a store of beads, feathers and shells, for instance. Keep a little bag or envelope with you when you are out and about – you never know what gems may be lying around the corner!

You will also be surprised what you can find stored away at home – old shirt buttons, antique lace, necklaces now out of fashion, belt buckles, broken bracelets and fittings on worn-out shoes. Seek and you will surely find something of creative worth for your cards!

Beads, buttons and charms These items, which can be sewn or glued on, come in an endless variety of colours, shapes, sizes and textures. Seed beads look great scattered and glued to the front of a card, to add highlights. Charms can be dangled from decorative threads, yarns or even wire.

Jewels and snowflakes Self-adhesive plastic crystal jewels, in a variety of shapes and rich colours, are available for bringing a touch of glitz and glamour to stamped images (see pages 76 and 83), while delicate diamanté and Diamond Dots, in a range of sizes, add sparkling highlights (see pages 74–75). Snowflake Frost A Peels come in different eye-catching patterns and are ideal for instantly embellishing festive cards (see pages 68–69).

Ribbons Never has there been such an amazing choice of ribbons. Ranging from pastel colours to vivid, ornate and printed, they add a feel of luxury to a greetings card. They come in fabric or paper in a variety of widths. Sheer ribbon is lovely for a light, romantic touch, such as for wedding themes. Satin ribbon is great for baby, birthday and men's cards. Raffia is ideal for ethnic or animal designs and for stringing tags.

Decorative yarns and threads These come in a wonderful array of colours and textures such as coarse, smooth, knobbly and with metallic threads running through. They are useful for attaching beads and charms, and for stringing tags.

Wire This adds movement to a card and comes in a range of bright metallic colours and different thicknesses or gauges. Bent with pliers or shaped into coils around a pencil, you can create hair (see page 82), messages, flowers, leaves and stars. Miniature wire coathangers are also fun to use (see page 83).

TIP

Wire stems can be flattened with a craft hammer after being shaped. This makes it easier to glue them to the card, and gives a different look.

Flowers, leaves, seedpods and twigs You can gather and press flowers and leaves from the garden (do not pick plant material from the wild); seedpods also make interesting additions to cards. Even humble twigs can be put to effective use, bound to a card with wire (see pages 64 and 80).

TIP

Avoid raiding beaches for shells – reputable craft shops and specialist suppliers offer a great variety to suit your needs.

Feathers and shells These are some of nature's own embellishments, which can be incorporated into your designs. Feathers in all kinds of colours and sizes are available from craft suppliers.

Making Multiples

I am always asked if there is a quick and easy way to make a series of cards of the same design, for example for wedding invitations, new baby announcement cards, new address cards or Christmas cards. Forward planning and streamlining the operation are the secrets of success, so here are a few practical tips to help you get geared up for the production line:

1 It is crucially important to make up a single example of the card design first so that you can work backwards, assessing which tools are needed for each stage, and also what materials and their quantities.

2 If a card has to be measured and cut to a certain size, do this first for all the cards. You will remember the measurements and get into a rhythm with the cutting. If you are using bought ready-folded card 'blanks', make sure you have all you need before you start, plus some spares in case you make mistakes, to avoid running short and not being able to obtain more of the same.

3 The new-style transparent polymer stamps (see page 14) are particularly useful for producing large batches of cards, as several different images can be combined on one large acrylic block to create a complete design that can be stamped all together.

4 If you are using brush markers or dye-based inks, ink up all the cards one after the other at one go. This saves you time getting materials in and out and keeps your work space uncluttered. As you finish one step, you can clear away the tools and materials involved and move on to the next. However, with embossed designs, each card needs to be inked and then embossing powder applied before moving on to the next – see pages 78–79 for further details.

5 Make sure you have all the embellishments you need for all the cards, and prepare and attach them all in one stage, such as cutting lengths of ribbon and tying, or gluing on buttons.

Turn to page 78 to see how to make multiples of this elegant invitation card.

TIP

Above all, remember that the cards do not have to be identical – as they are handmade, each one will be subtly unique.

Try these designs for quantity with quality, such as the christening card (see page 93), variations on a Santa theme for Christmas (see page 80) and a wedding invitation (see page 95).

Brush Marker Blooms

You will need...

white glossy card
12.5x7.5cm (5x3in)

lime green spotted card
14.5x9.5cm (5¾x3¾in)

purple card blank
16x11cm (6¼x4¼in)

flower stems stamp

brush markers: purple and
leaf green

cotton bud

wet stamp cleaning pad or
kitchen paper

old towel

Brush markers were originally the only way to stamp, so stampers often regard them as outdated. But here you will see how professional a result can be achieved on gloss card.

Terrific value, brush markers are water-based brush pens that come in an array of colours and sizes. With a larger brush tip, you can rapidly colour in solid areas of the stamp, while a medium size enables you to colour directly onto the stamp or fill in the stamped image. Use a fine tip for colouring in small areas or for writing a coordinated message.

1 Colour in the flower stamp, applying brush markers directly onto the rubber. Use the purple marker for the flowers and leaf green for the stems and leaves.

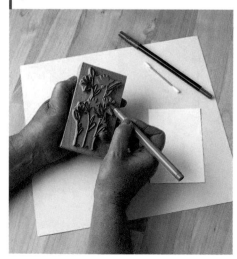

2 Clean off any excess ink from the background of the stamp with a cotton bud.

3 Carefully stamp centrally onto the white glossy card, taking care not to rock the stamp or allow it to slide across the card.

4 Lift off the stamp, holding the card firmly with your other hand.

TIP

To re-dampen the ink on the rubber if it dries before you have finished colouring it in, breathe heavily onto the inked area of the stamp.

5 Clean the stamp using a wet stamp cleaning pad or a double layer of well-dampened kitchen paper and dry it with an old towel.

To finish…

Mount the stamped flower card centrally onto the lime green spotted paper, then onto the purple card blank using double-sided tape.

A pear stamp was coloured with brush markers in lime, yellow, pale orange, burnt orange and moss green, then stamped out onto gloss card mounted onto orange card. To make the base card, a sprig leaf stamp was inked with two tones of green brush marker and randomly stamped onto gloss card – the pear card was adhered centrally onto this.

All the stamps were inked with an embossing pad and inked with brush markers. Swirls, spots and dragonflies were coloured hot pink and turquoise, stamped onto gloss card, sprinkled with clear embossing powder and heat embossed. For the central design, white gloss card was punched out with two sizes of square punch and stamped. The white card was mounted onto purple card, adhered to turquoise card, then to purple base card.

Tonal Leaves

white glossy card
12x6.5cm (4¾x2½in)

orange card
13.5x8cm (5½x3¼in)

moss green card blank
18x10.5cm (7x4¼in)

leaf pattern stamp

brush markers: orange, red,
yellow ochre and olive green

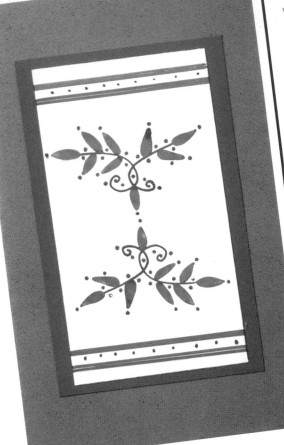

Now that you have all rushed out and bought your own brush markers, here is another project to put them to creative use, where a darker colour is dabbed onto areas of the design to give a toned effect.

This leaf design is reminiscent of the Art Nouveau period, and the rich colours are inspired by the pottery of Clarice Cliff. Remember to keep your eyes open for objects around you, from which you can draw ideas for your cards, and don't be afraid to experiment with colours and techniques.

1 Using the orange brush marker, colour in the leaves of the stamp directly onto the rubber.

2 Using the red brush marker, colour in only the area nearest to the stem on each leaf. This will give a toned look to the leaf, with the darker shade at the base and the lighter at the tip.

3 Dab the yellow ochre brush marker over the leaves at random to enrich the colour. Carefully colour in the decorative stem and dots with the olive green brush marker. Breathe onto the stamp to keep the ink damp.

4 Stamp firmly onto the white card, aligning the central leaf with the centre of the card, taking care not to rock the stamp on contact with the card.

5 Lift off the stamp, holding the card firmly with your other hand.

6 Repeat steps 1–3, then turn the stamp around, as shown. Stamp the design directly above, and in line with, the first stamped image and carefully lift off. Trim the card to size, if necessary.

The leaf design was coloured with aqua blue, sea green and purple brush markers, stamped onto glossy card, then covered with striped vellum, anchored with lilac eyelets (see page 49).

TIP
Start colouring with the lightest brush markers first, moving down the scale to the darkest. This helps to keep the tips of each brush clean.

To finish…
Using a ruler, draw two parallel lines in orange and red across the top and bottom of the card, cleaning off the ruler between colours. Apply olive green dots, at random, between the lines. Mount onto orange card, then onto the moss green card blank using double-sided tape.

Shadow-Stamped Stem

You will need...

stone card
14x7.5cm (5½x3in)

grey card blank
15x9cm (6x3½in)

three-squared foam block
shadow stamp

flower foam block stamp

shadow ink cubes™:
soft teal and soft leaf

purple brush marker

Shadow stamping offers new ways to create subtle backgrounds using solid colours. Squares and oblongs are among the most popular shapes, but any solid background shape is suitable.

It is important to use soft pastel colours for shadow stamping, which are provided by special inks. These permanent dye-based inks do not bleed and are available in a wide range of subdued shades.

There are many creative ways to employ shadow stamping, so take time to stretch your imagination.

Even a practice piece of stamping need not go to waste – here, the image was torn around, mounted and a raffia-tied gift tag added to continue the recycled theme.

1 Apply the soft teal ink cube to the three-squared stamp using a dabbing action. Then, with the leading edge of the ink cube, score lightly through the inked area to create a streaked effect when stamped.

2 Firmly press the stamp centrally onto the stone card, keeping the pressure even all over.

White card was coloured with alternating brush marker colours, over-stamped with a flower stamp, then mounted onto a coordinating background card.

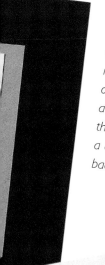

3 Colour the flower stem and petals of the flower stamp with the soft leaf ink cube, then colour the flower with a purple brush marker.

TIP

To give a 'negative' image, ink your shadow stamp, then draw on dots, lines or hearts with a paintbrush before stamping. This removes the ink to give the negative image.

This card was first stamped with shadow stamps in varying sizes and shapes in soft peach ink, then over-stamped with different leaf motifs in soft leaf ink.

4 Carefully stamp the flower centrally over the stamped squares, holding the card when lifting off the stamp.

Pencil Blended Bookmark

This coloured-pencil project – a greetings card that incorporates a gift bookmark – harks back to those good old schooldays of 'colouring in', and it is still one of the most relaxing art techniques.

The best type of pencils to use are wax based. They have a soft pigment lead that particularly lends itself to blending – combining colours that tone with each other to create new shades. Keep the pencils sharp with a good sharpener.

Bear in mind, when it comes to applying colour, that light falls first on the top of a tree or flower, so it will be lighter than the bottom portion.

You will need...

white matt card 30x5.5cm (12x2¼in)

forest green card blank 20x10.5cm (8x4¼in)

transparent daisy and three-squares stamp and acrylic block 14x10cm (5½x4in)

black permanent ink pad

wax coloured pencils: yellow, orange, lime green, olive green, coral and crimson

dimensional magic™

¼in holepunch

1.5cm (⅝in) wide sheer ribbon: orange and yellow

magnetic strip

1 Lightly mark the halfway point on the strip of white card with a pencil. Position the stamp on the acrylic block. Ink the stamp using a black permanent ink pad and stamp centrally onto the lower half of the card. Lift off the stamp, holding the card. Clean the stamp and allow to dry thoroughly before colouring.

2 Start colouring the daisy petals using the yellow pencil at the top of the petals, then the orange below (see facing page).

3 Colour in the leaves using lime green pencil on the top portion, blending to olive green below. Highlight the daisy petals with coral pencil and colour in the centre with crimson pencil.

4 To emphasize the impression of depth, apply Dimensional Magic™ to the base of the petals with a paintbrush and allow to dry for 30 minutes.

TIP

If you do not have a permanent ink pad, use a pigment ink pad and emboss with clear powder. Be careful not to chip the embossing with the coloured pencils.

5 Score the card in half widthways using a bone folder. Fold, then punch a hole through both front and back card pieces. Thread ribbons through the holes and tie.

6 Cut two lengths of magnetic strip and glue along the bottom edges inside the card. With a craft knife held against a ruler, carefully cut a slit 5.5cm (2¼in) long 2.5cm (1in) from the top front of the green card blank. Insert the back of the bookmark through the slit.

Blending

To blend the colours, press the yellow pencil hard into the card, working back and forth over a small area. Then continue with the orange pencil over the adjacent area. Go back to the area where the two colours join and work the orange pencil in a small circular movement into the yellow area, pressing hard to mash the pigment wax together to blend the colours. Repeat, working the yellow pencil into the orange area.

Water-Brushed Framed Flower

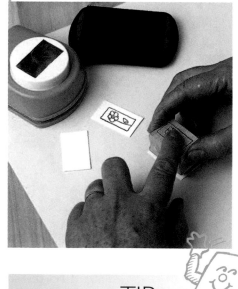

This vibrant card features the basic technique of watercolour painting using dye-based ink pads. The design and approach may be simple, but the results are impactful and literally unique! Water is the key medium, which controls the depth and density of the colour, so the finished effect can be quite unpredictable.

It is a good idea to punch or cut out several rectangles of card for painting so that you can experiment and practise first. You can keep the best practise pieces for incorporating into other card designs.

You will need…

sheet of watercolour card

lime green card
5x3.5cm (2x1½in)

white matt card blank
12cm (4¾in) square

single daisy stamp

black pigment ink pad

vivid™ dye-based ink pads:
raspberry, orange, spring
green and aqua

clear embossing powder

punch for cutting
4x2.25cm (1½x¾in)
rectangles

heat gun

kitchen foil

paper heart border sticker

1 Using the craft punch, punch out several rectangles of watercolour card so that you have some spares to practice on. Ink the stamp with a black pigment ink pad and firmly stamp centrally onto the card.

2 Sprinkle clear embossing powder over the wet image and tap off the excess powder.

TIP

**Make sure you use
watercolour card
so that it does not
buckle when wet.**

3 Holding the stamped card with the end of a paintbrush or similar tool, direct a heat gun over the image. Watch for all the powder to melt so that you will be left with a black shiny raised image. The resulting embossed area will work as a resist to the water and inks.

4 Fold a sheet of kitchen foil into three and open out. Press each dye-based ink pad firmly onto the middle section of the foil to leave an ink residue. (When you have finished, fold in the outer sections of foil and store for future use.)

5 Using a large paintbrush, brush the stamped card liberally with water outside the image frame. Then, with a wet finer brush, pick up ink from the foil and drop onto the wet area. Alternate colours and watch them spread into each other. Clean the brush between colours.

6 With your clean wet fine brush, colour in the daisy flower and leaf. Leave to dry.

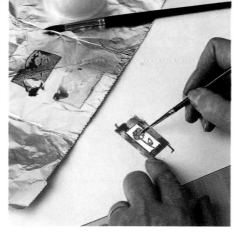

7 Mount the lime green card centrally onto the white card blank with double-sided tape, then centrally mount the painted card on top.

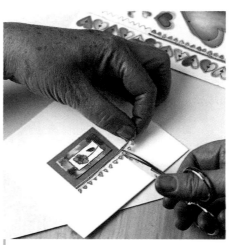

8 Cut two 5cm (2in) lengths of heart border sticker and position either side of the lime green card. You could add your own greeting under the design to finish.

Sponged Butterfly Backdrop

Sponging is a wonderfully useful and versatile technique, yet fun to do and easy enough to involve children. Sponged backgrounds can be over-stamped with coordinating coloured inks, or try sponging over a flower mask (see pages 38–39) or a peel-off motif to create a silhouetted image. Artistically sponged skies and meadows can create appealingly atmospheric designs. Brilliance™ pigment ink pads, as used here, give an attractive pearlized finish.

You can also use sponging to cover up mistakes or to transform garishly coloured cut-price card into designer stationery.

You will need...

- pale pink card
  7cm (2¾in) square
- grey card blank
  13cm (5in) square
- pale green card
  7cm (2¾in) square
- butterfly stamp
- spiral flower head stamp
- black pigment ink pad
- brilliance™ ink pads: lime green, purple, lavender and pink
- acrylic paints: purple, pink, blue and green
- clear embossing powder
- heat gun
- sponge

I Ink all over the butterfly stamp with a black pigment ink pad using a dabbing action. Firmly stamp diagonally onto the centre of the pale pink card, then carefully lift off the stamp, holding the card. Clean the stamp.

2 Sprinkle clear embossing powder over the wet image and tap off the excess powder.

3 Direct a heat gun at the image and move it back and forth evenly across the design until the image is raised and shiny.

4 Colour in the butterfly using acrylic paints and a wet paintbrush. Set aside to dry.

TIP

Rinse sponges in soapy water, then rinse. Squeeze out the excess water and wrap in clingfilm to prevent them drying out and hardening.

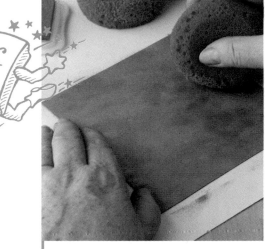

5 Dab a sponge onto a lime green ink pad, then randomly over the grey card blank. Repeat with purple ink and finish off with lavender. Leave to dry or direct a heat gun over the sponged area, moving it back and forth across the card.

6 Ink the flower stamp with a pink ink pad using a dabbing action. Firmly stamp at random over the sponged card. Clean the stamp and repeat with lime green ink. Clean the stamp again and leave the card to dry.

TRY THIS

Centre a self-adhesive note on an envelope. Sponge all over the surrounding area with the same colours used on the card. Remove the mask to reveal a plain area for the address. Ink the flower stamp with pink ink and randomly stamp over the sponged area, stamping halfway into the plain area at the top right- and bottom left-hand corners for added interest.

7 Mount the pale green card, centred, onto the sponged card blank, then mount the butterfly-stamped card diagonally in the centre.

Spiral Daisy Photo Frame

You will need…

tri-fold cream card blank
17x12cm (6¾x4¾in) with a
5cm (2in) square aperture

spiral daisies stamp

black pigment ink pad

self-adhesive note

clear embossing powder

heat gun

A ny grandparent would treasure a charmingly framed photograph of their grandchild to keep and display. Fortunately, you do not have to be an expert to create such a family heirloom.

The secret of success here is to keep the stamping understated both in design and colour, so that it complements the portrait rather than competing with it for attention. This stamp design is a classic – one that is always sure to work and delight.

1 Cover up the aperture of the card with a self-adhesive note, positioning it just beyond the edge of the top left-hand corner. Ink the stamp with a black pigment ink pad using a dabbing action. Working over scrap paper, firmly stamp onto the top left-hand corner of the card, stamping over the edge. Carefully lift off the stamp.

2 Peel away the note to reveal the framed corner.

3 Sprinkle clear embossing powder over the wet image and tap off the excess powder.

4 Direct a heat gun at the stamped image and move it back and forth evenly across the design. Continue applying heat until the image is raised and shiny.

TIP

Before heating, check that no embossing powder has dropped through the aperture into the folded card – brush away any specks with a paintbrush.

5 Cover up the card aperture again, this time with a self-adhesive note positioned just beyond the edge of the bottom right-hand corner. Re-ink the stamp with black pigment ink and stamp firmly onto the right-hand corner of the card.

6 Lift off the stamp, holding the card. Remove the note. Sprinkle clear embossing powder over the wet image, tap off the excess, then emboss with the heat gun as instructed in Step 4.

TRY THIS

Stamp and emboss a matching envelope with the same spiral daisies stamp. Remember to clean the stamp thoroughly.

7 Glue the photograph in place behind the aperture using an archival (acid-free) glue to avoid damaging the photograph. Glue down the edges of the tri-fold card so that it becomes an ordinary single-folded card.

Multi-Inked Maple Leaves

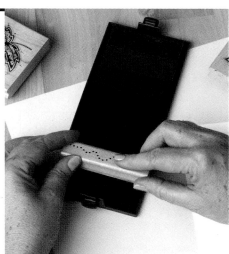

You will need...

- white glossy card blank 18x13cm (7x5in), used horizontally
- scrap of white glossy card
- dotted line stamp
- large dotted maple leaf stamp
- small dotted maple leaf stamp
- multicoloured dye-based ink pad
- ⅛in holepunch
- medium orange wire

Once you have tried one, you will wonder how you ever got along without a state-of-the-art multicoloured ink pad. Available in a spectacular range of colours, this particular variety is dye based and is best for stamping on glossy card and other non-absorbent materials.

These pads are ideal for producing a card when time is short, as the ink dries rapidly on a glossy surface and reproduces the finest lines of a rubber-stamped image with professional clarity. The colours used here were chosen to reflect the rich range of hues in falling autumnal leaves.

1 Holding the dotted line stamp firmly, press onto the green area of the multicoloured ink pad. Check that the entire image is covered with ink (the rubber will glisten when inked).

2 Place the stamp parallel to the left-hand edge of the card blank and press down. Carefully remove the stamp while holding the card to avoid blurring the image. Re-ink the stamp and stamp, lining up with the first image to reach the edge of the card.

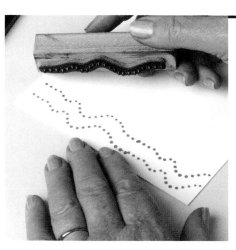

3 Re-ink the stamp on the red section of the ink pad and stamp parallel to the green dotted line. Re-ink and stamp again to complete the line as before.

4 Holding the large leaf stamp firmly, press onto an area of your choice on the ink pad. Slowly move the stamp backwards and press down again to stop a hard line forming across the image when stamped.

5 Stamp firmly onto the right-hand side of card and carefully lift off, holding the card. Clean the stamp.

TIP

To give a professional finish, try stamping over the edge of the card. Always have the card on a piece of scrap paper to avoid staining your work surface.

6 Repeat on the left-hand side of the card, then use the smaller leaf stamp to complete the design. Making sure that you have a piece of scrap paper under the card, stamp a couple of small leaves over the card edge.

To finish…

Stamp a small leaf on a scrap of card and cut out. Punch two holes side by side through the leaf and the front of the main card in the top left-hand corner. Thread wire through the holes, with the ends emerging from the front. Thread on sequins, then twist the wire ends around a thin pencil to coil.

A magnolia-design stamp was inked using a multi-ink pad and stamped onto gloss card. A small tag was then cut out to carry a message such as 'Get Well' or 'Thank You'. A tiny hole was punched either side of the stem and the tag attached. The design was mounted onto folded navy base card to finish.

Multi-Inked Maple Leaves **31**

Fancy Frames

All kinds of decorative borders and frames can be created to give added interest to your stamping work when mounted.

Some stamp designs particularly lend themselves to being cut out with fancy-edged scissors, and there are many different types available to experiment with. Try cutting two parallel lines to create a lacy border.

Leaves and other shapes can be punched or cut out and arranged around a stamped image, attached with 3-D foam pads. Sticker borders in a multitude of patterns and colours are another effective way of framing.

glossy white card, slightly larger than the stamp design

scraps of coral and purple card

gift token card 21x10cm (8¼x4in) and envelope

garden sampler stamp

multicoloured dye-based ink pad

purple liquid pearls™

deckle-edged scissors

daisy punch

punch for cutting 1cm (⅜in) squares

multicoloured threads

1 Position the stamp over the colours of the multicoloured dye-based ink pad that you want to use. Lightly tap the stamp a few times onto the surface of the pad.

2 Firmly stamp onto white card. Carefully lift off the stamp, holding the card.

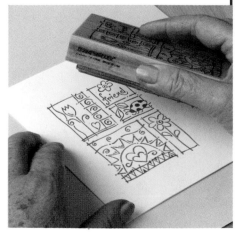

3 Using deckle-edged scissors, cut between the different sections of the stamped design.

4 Mount the separate pieces of the design onto coral and purple card using double-sided tape. Cut around the edge of each piece using the deckle-edged scissors, leaving a 3mm (⅛in) border of coloured card.

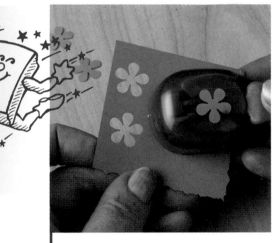

TIP

For a quick and easy border, use a decorative punch to punch out a strip of card, spacing the punch evenly as you go.

5 Punch out four daisies and three squares from purple card, then punch out four daisies and three squares from coral card.

6 Glue the coral daisies to the purple squares and the purple daisies to the coral squares. Glue the two remaining daisies to the 'friends' tag. Mount the stamped images onto the gift token card with double-sided tape, referring to the finished card as a guide to positioning.

7 Glue the daisy squares to the card in two rows of three as shown in the finished card. Add a drop of purple Liquid Pearls™ to the flower centres. Leave to dry for 20 minutes.

8 Thread multicoloured threads through the hole in the gift token card and glue the tag onto the flap.

Bleached Sunflower Label

You will need...

black card
16x9cm (6x3½in)

cream card
16x9cm (6x3½in)

brown card blank
16.5x9cm (6½x3½in)
and cream envelope

sunflower label stamp

clear embossing ink pad

gold embossing powder

heat gun

household bleach

heavy ceramic container

¼in holepunch

1.5cm (⅝in) wide sheer
ribbon: cream and coffee

This sunflower design lends itself perfectly to the technique of bleaching, worked on a contrasting black background. The tonal effect is achieved by bleaching some areas more than others. You can also dip your stamp directly into bleach for stamping, but take care not to drip any bleach onto clothing or furnishings.

Place the bleach in a heavy ceramic container and stand in a tray, in case it should get knocked over. Wash your hands and any brushes directly after use and remove the bleach from your work table as soon as you have finished the project. Now lighten your day!

1 Ink the stamp thoroughly with the embossing pad by dabbing over the rubber image and making sure that it is glistening all over. Stamp onto the black card, taking care not to rock the stamp. Carefully lift off, holding the card.

2 Sprinkle gold embossing powder over the wet image. Tap off the excess powder. Remove any unwanted gold specks with a paintbrush.

3 Direct a heat gun at the image and move it back and forth evenly across the design until the image is raised and shiny. Do not overheat the powder or it will dull.

4 The raised image makes it easy for you to apply the bleach. Carefully pour bleach into a heavy ceramic container. Using a paintbrush, apply bleach to areas of the design that you want to lighten.

TIP
Embossing helps to stop the bleach spreading. But if it does spread a little, or you drip a little bleach, it will only add to the card's character.

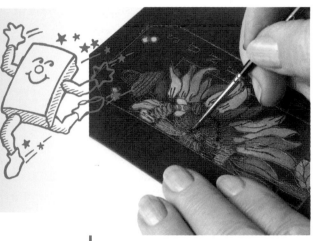

5 To create the tonal effect, apply more bleach to some already bleached areas to lighten them further. Continue bleaching until the required effect is achieved.

To finish…
Cut around the sunflower frame, leaving a 5mm (¼in) border all round. Mount onto cream card with double-sided tape and trim to leave a 5mm (¼in) border all round. Punch a hole at the top, thread through ribbon, then mount onto the brown card blank.

This collection of tags was created using the same sunflower stamp design and bleaching technique on different card colours – the bleach acts slightly differently on each colour.

TRY THIS
Embellish an envelope to match using a stencilled tag motif stamped with copper-coloured flowers, and add details with a gold gel pen.

Resist-Ink Tapestry

white glossy card
13x10cm (5x4in)

white glossy card blank
13x10cm (5x4in)

moth stamp

versamark™ resist-ink pad

multicoloured dye-based
ink pad

heat gun

brayer

wide decorative ribbon

small butterfly punch

The wonderfully textured effect of this card was achieved by stamping a moth image in resist ink on white glossy card. As in the project on page 30, a multicoloured ink pad then works its magic, but here the ink is applied using a brayer – a roller – over the whole surface of the card (see page 6). The stamped images emerge in the white of the base card, having resisted the ink.

Experience the creative results of this captivating technique – you will find that no two pieces of work are the same. Time to start brayering!

1 Holding the stamp firmly, press onto the resist-ink pad, then onto the single piece of white card. Repeat until several images cover the card. Use a heat gun to thoroughly dry the stamped images. The ink may give off a little smoke while drying, but this is normal.

2 Roller the whole brayer over the orange area of the ink pad, then roller across the card, with a protective layer of scrap paper underneath. Add pressure to the roller to work the ink into the card. Ensure you roller off the edges to achieve even distribution. Clean the brayer.

3 If you have an especially wet ink pad, wipe over the card with a piece of kitchen paper to remove any excess ink – the moth images will show even more clearly.

4 Repeat Step 1 to build up the design. You could, if you wanted, introduce a different stamp at this stage to vary the design.

TIP
When brayering, move over the card with even strokes, starting and ending a little away from the card to avoid making lines.

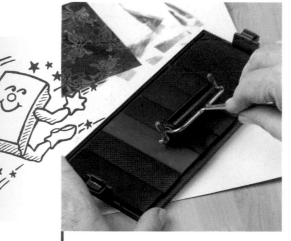

5 Ink up the brayer with a different colour from the ink pad to give depth to your card. This is where the unexpected happens – the fun part of the technique.

6 Roller across the entire surface of the card as in Step 2 and wipe off any excess ink with kitchen paper.

7 Glue a length of ribbon across the lower half of the card. Punch out six butterflies from a practice piece of brayered card and glue together back to back.

To finish…
Mount the brayered card onto the card blank, then the butterflies with double-sided tape, lifting up their wings to give a 3-D effect.

Fading Flowers

white glossy card blank
12x9cm (4¾x3½in),
with 2cm (¾in) trimmed off
the front edge

daisy head stamp

brush markers: lime green,
yellow, orange and turquoise

self-adhesive note

ball sponge

B y using a masking technique with overlapping stamped designs, you can create an intriguing spatial effect, with images fading away behind others. For example, if you stamp a butterfly onto card, cover it with a cutout 'mask' of the image, then stamp a flower image over the mask, when you remove the mask the butterfly will appear as if resting on the flower. A collection of balloons one behind another, tied to a cat's tail, would also look effective.

Masks take a long time to cut out, so store them stuck, with repositional glue, in a small, labelled notebook.

1 Colour the stamp with a brush marker. Stamp the image as close as possible to the top front of a self-adhesive note, to make use of the sticky strip on the back. Clean the stamp well.

2 Carefully cut out the daisy image, trimming neatly around the edge, to make the mask.

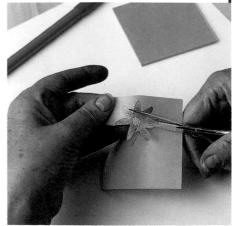

3 Colour in the daisy stamp, beginning with the lightest colour – lime green.

4 Colour around the centre of the daisy with the yellow brush marker, then the orange, just dabbing here and there. Breathe onto the stamp to keep the ink damp. Firmly stamp onto the centre of the card and lift off carefully, holding the card in place. Clean the stamp well.

TIP

Stamps must be kept clean when using brush markers. If they are very dirty, use a baby wipe, then clean off any ink residue.

5 Cover the stamped image with the mask. Colour in the daisy stamp, again starting with the lime green brush marker, then yellow and orange, occasionally adding a turquoise streak. Dampen the ink by breathing heavily onto it and stamp over the right-hand side of the mask.

6 Carefully lift off the stamp, holding the card firmly. Clean the stamp again thoroughly.

7 Lift off the mask to reveal the second stamped daisy image behind the first.

8 Make a second mask so that you can build up an area of overlapping daisies, colouring the stamp as in Step 5, until the design is completed. Keep cleaning off the brush markers by scribbling onto scrap paper.

9 Open up the card and mask the inside back with a spare piece of card, leaving a 2cm (¾in) wide margin along the right-hand edge. Ink a ball sponge with an orange brush marker and dab over the unmasked area. Repeat with yellow, then green brush marker.

10 Using a ruler, draw a vertical line centrally down the sponged strip with the yellow brush marker, then another line to the left with the orange brush marker, cleaning the ruler between the different colours.

11 Use the point of the lime green brush marker to add leaf shapes at alternating points along either side of the lines.

TRY THIS
Change the theme of a card by using different features and embellishments. The Easter Bunny card (see facing page, top) would work equally well as a birth announcement with the addition of baby accessories instead of Easter eggs (see pages 92–93 and the other galleries for inspiration).

A bunny stamp was inked using a
black permanent ink pad and stamped
centrally onto white matt card. This
first image was masked, the bunny
stamped to the right and left, then
the mask removed. The bow ties
were coloured and the bunnies
embellished with glitter before being
mounted on to spotted background
paper, then onto purple card.
Cut-out Easter eggs and daisies
provided the finishing touches.

A butterfly was stamped and masked, then a rose
stamped over the top. The rose was masked and
stamped again to the left. With both roses masked,
leaves were stamped as shown. The mask was
removed and the images coloured using pencils,
blending the shades. Another butterfly was stamped
out on a piece of scrap card, coloured and cut out. This
was 3-D'd over the first butterfly (see page 42), lifting
the wings up, then the design was mounted.

Starting at the left of the card, a
zebra was stamped and masked,
then a second zebra stamped
over the first, twisted upwards
to give movement. This was
repeated until all four zebras
were stamped. Using the
zebra mask again, foliage was
stamped over the zebras.
Mount as shown.

3-D Red Nosed Rudolph

Three-dimensional découpage has been an incredibly popular craft for many years. Here, the same approach is applied to stamped images rather than printed images to create a comparable effect. This simple yet highly effective technique literally adds another dimension to your stamping work. The biggest challenge is in neatly cutting out the images. You can use either a small, sharp pair of scissors or a craft knife working on a cutting mat, depending on what you feel most comfortable with.

1 Using a dabbing action, ink the stamp all over with a very wet black pigment ink pad. Firmly stamp three evenly spaced images onto the suede paper strip, re-inking the stamp each time. Stamp six more images on spare suede paper – they can be stamped close together to conserve the paper.

2 Colour in all the images with coloured pencils referring to the finished card as a guide.

3 Take three of the spare reindeer images and cut around the antlers, ears and through the top of the nose, just below the eyes.

4 Attach 3-D foam pads to the back of the cutouts. Turn over and if any of the foam pads show, colour in the foam with fawn brush marker.

TIP

If you find the cutting out difficult and leave a fawn border in places, simply colour it in with a black pen – no one will know!

5 Stick down the three cutouts onto the three original stamped images on the suede paper strip.

6 Take the remaining three reindeer images and cut out the antlers and ears only. Attach 3-D foam pads and stick down on the suede paper strip as in Step 5.

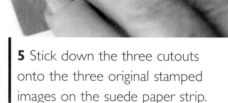

7 Thread two 21cm (8¼in) lengths of ribbon through a Xyron™ sticker machine following the manufacturer's instructions, to dispense glue evenly onto the ribbon, or use a glue spreader to apply glue.

8 Mount the suede paper strip, centring it horizontally, onto the green card blank using double-sided tape. Cover the top and bottom edges with the ribbon. Glue a red pompon to each nose.

Chalk Checks

You will need…

A4 or US letter sheet of white paper

blue paper
11x9cm (4½x3½in)

sheet of white card

grey card blank
12x10cm (4¾x4in)

flower trio stamp

thin and thick grid line stencils
(or use the template on page 101)

palette of decorating chalks

purple glitter gel pen

black permanent ink pad

cotton wool balls and cotton bud

Chalks come in a palette ranging from dreamy pastels to vibrant shades and warm, earthy tones. Choose colours to create a particular mood or setting for your card.

The beauty of chalks is their ability to blend together for a soft and subtle finish. Purpose-made sponge applicators are best for enhancing the intensity of the colours, but chalks can also be applied with cotton wool or buds and a dry fine paintbrush for detailed work.

A special soft chalk eraser allows you to tidy up your work by rubbing away any smudges.

1 Place the thin grid line stencil over white paper. Dab a cotton wool ball into blue chalk. Holding the stencil firmly, dab the cotton wool along the grid lines, building up the colour.

2 You can at any time pull back the stencil to check your work, making sure that your other hand holds it in place. If you find that the stencil moves when chalking, spray the back lightly with stencil (repositional) adhesive to hold it in place.

3 Overlay the thick (wide) grid line stencil at right angles to the blue chalk lines. This time, dab along the lines with green chalk.

4 With a purple glitter gel pen draw freehand or use the outside of the stencil or a ruler to draw a grid of intersecting lines centrally through the palest strips of the design, creating a bold check.

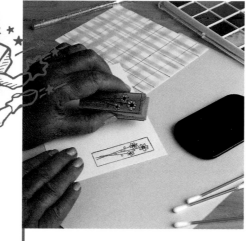

5 Ink the flower trio stamp with a black permanent ink pad and stamp onto white card.

6 Use a cotton bud to colour in the flower design with chalks.

The two larger glossy heart tags were coated in Versmark™ ink (one through a home-made 'dotty' stencil, the other coated directly) then dusted with hot-pink chalk, coated with Versmark™ and clear embossed. The third, smaller, glossy tag was stamped with a decorative stamp, using black pigment ink, clear embossed, coloured with brush markers, and edged in pink. The tags were mounted as shown.

To finish…
Trim the white paper to 10x7cm (4x2¾in) and the stamped card to 8x4cm (3¼x1½in). Mount the stamped card centrally onto the checked background paper and then onto the blue paper and grey card blank with double-sided tape.

Translucent Dragonfly

pearlized teal card blank
12cm (4¾in) square

sheet of vellum paper with
gold and silver flecks

scrap of turquoise
water-like paper

dragonfly and reeds stamp

versamark™ resist-ink pad

palette of decorating chalks

cotton wool balls

soft chalk eraser

4x⅛in purple eyelets

⅛in eyelet holepunch and
fixing tool

craft hammer

Two excellent materials – chalk and resist ink – are teamed together to bring a suitably diffused, watery feel to this lakeside scene. Here, the resist ink is used to adhere the chalk, and the whole effect is further enhanced by using vellum paper. This combination also produces a soft look on matt card, as in the variation.

Resist ink can also be used to create a watermark effect, like the delicate watermarks you find in handmade papers. See the main project on pages 70–73, where a daisy pattern stamped with resist ink onto a pale pink card (step 7) appears in a subtly darker shade.

1 Ink the stamp with the resist-ink pad. Make sure that the entire rubber image glistens to indicate that the stamp has been thoroughly inked.

2 Firmly stamp in the right-hand corner of the vellum paper, lining up the stamp with the edge. This makes trimming easier. Carefully lift off the stamp, holding the vellum in place – this ink is fairly sticky until it dries. Clean the stamp.

3 Dab a cotton wool ball into lime green chalk, then dab over the reeds and the lower half of the outside frame.

4 Dab a fresh cotton wool ball into purple chalk, then dab over the top half of the frame.

TIP

A piece of scrap paper placed under your hand when chalking will help to prevent chalk smudges.

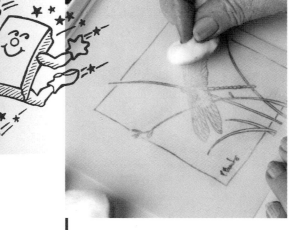

5 Dab another fresh cotton wool ball into aqua blue chalk, then partially dab over the dragonfly wings. Use purple, then lime green chalk to vary the colour.

6 If you have an excess of chalk powder, either blow it away or carefully brush it away with a soft dry paintbrush.

7 Use a soft chalk eraser to remove any chalk smudges.

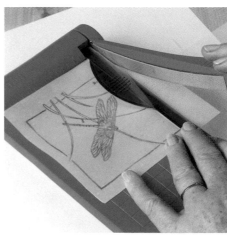

8 Trim your artwork, leaving a 1cm (⅜in) border of vellum around the framed image.

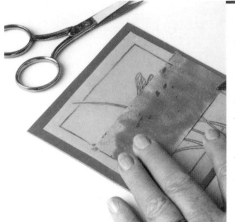

9 Measure and mark out a strip of the water-like paper to run behind the dragonfly and fit horizontally within the frame. Cut out. Place the vellum centrally on the card blank and mark the positioning of the strip, so that the dragonfly will appear to fly over the watery strip.

10 Remove the vellum and stick the paper strip in place on the base card with double-sided tape. Fix a purple eyelet in each corner of the vellum panel, following the instructions given on the facing page.

A daisy was stamped onto orange vellum using Versamark™, then the wet image dusted with orange and red chalks. The spotted background was made using the tip of a brush marker on glossy card. An eyelet fixed the daisy to the background, which was then adhered to burnt orange card.

A leaf sampler design was resist-inked, stamped onto two pieces of cream card and dusted with chalks. One main image and sections from the second image were cut out, arranged and mounted.

FIXING EYELETS

Eyelets can fix pieces of card together or be purely decorative. They are available in two sizes – ⅛in and ³⁄₁₆in – and a range of colours and shapes. You will need a punch to match the size of the eyelet with a round, hollow tip at the end that cuts a hole through the paper or card, a fixing tool and a hammer to tap the punch and fixing tool, plus a cutting mat to protect your work surface.

Other decorative ways to use eyelets:

- as centres of flowers
- as buttons on clothes
- to make wheels on cars
- to attach a series of square paper tiles bearing initials or a message, such as 'Good Luck'
- to make holes for threading ribbons through, for example in a row as a border
- to make holes for threading wire through at the bottom of a card, on which to hang charms (see tag, below centre)

1 Position the two papers to be fixed together. Hold the punch vertically and tap the end with a hammer to punch a hole through all the layers (usually two sharp taps will be sufficient). Insert an eyelet through each hole from the front. Turn the work over.

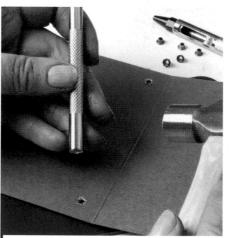

2 Insert the fixing tool into the eyelet hole. Tap the fixing tool with a hammer (again, two sharp taps). To eliminate rough edges, remove the fixing tool and tap the back of the eyelet with the hammer.

The decorative tags shown left demonstrate how eyelets can be used creatively to embellish even the simplest of shapes and materials.

Creative Craft Combo

You will need...

bright blue card blank
14cm (5½in) square

white card
10.5x5.5cm (4¼x2¼in),
plus extra for the tag

dark blue card
11x6cm (4½x2½in)

gold card
11.5x6.5cm (4¾x2¾in)

pink, yellow and
patterned paper

sheet of acetate

border daisy head stamp

large daisy head stamp

palette of decorating chalks

dye-based ink pads: dark
blue and yellow

gold leaf and green pens

gold liquid pearls™

self-adhesive note

daisy and plant pot
punches

texture yarns

3-D foam pads

You will have endless fun exercising all your crafty skills in creating this arty card. This design brings together four major techniques – punching, mounting, using decorating chalks and, of course, stamping – and shows what interesting results can be achieved by using different approaches in combination.

However, if you want or need to take a short cut, use a decorative background paper for the base card chosen from the wide variety that is available, instead of chalking and stamping the pattern onto the card.

1 Use the template on page 101 to cut a stencil from acetate. Line up the medium grid line horizontally about 1.5cm (⅝in) from the bottom of the blue card blank. Dab a cotton wool ball into royal blue chalk, then evenly along the grid line.

2 Repeat with the thin grid line 5mm (¼in) above the chalked line.

3 Repeat with the wide grid line 1.5cm (⅝in) from the card top. Repeat with the stencil vertical and the medium grid line 1cm (⅜in) from the right-hand edge. Repeat with the extra-wide grid line 2cm (¾in) away from the right-hand edge.

4 Stamp the daisy border in dark blue ink down the left- and right-hand side of the widest chalk line, re-inking between stamping. Stamp the large daisy head in yellow ink along the right-hand and top edges.

5 Colour the extra-wide grid line 7.5mm (⅛in) from the left-hand edge of the white card with pale blue chalk. Repeat with the medium grid line 3.5cm (1½in) from the left-hand edge and the thin grid line in yellow chalk 1cm (⅜in) from the right-hand edge and with the stencil horizontal 1.5cm (⅝in) from the top-edge medium grid lines and along the bottom edge. Complete the stamping as on the finished card.

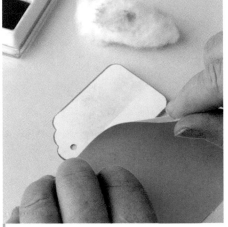

6 Cut out a tag from white card using the template on page 100. Place a self-adhesive note 5mm (¼in) below the tag hole and dab lightly with blue chalk. Remove the note and place over the chalked area, then dab the remaining area with yellow chalk. Highlight the tag edges with a gold leaf pen.

7 Using two different daisy punches, or a single punch, punch out two daisies from pink paper and one from yellow paper. Punch out three pots from patterned paper. Add a drop of gold Liquid Pearls™ in the centre of each flower and allow to dry for 20 minutes. Attach the flowers and pots in a row on the tag with double-sided tape. Draw in stems and leaves with green pen.

To finish…

Mount the white card onto the dark blue card, then mount onto the gold card using double-sided tape. Mount this panel 2cm (¾in) from the left-hand edge of the decorated blue card, centring vertically. Thread the tag with texture yarns and mount centrally onto the card with 3-D foam pads.

Gold Embossed Pansy

You will need...

white card
9.5x5.5cm (3¾x2¼in)

purple card
11x10cm (4½x4in)

lime green card blank
13cm (5¼in) square

small triangle of purple
patterned and textured paper

pansy and frame stamp

clear embossing ink pad

gold embossing powder

watercolour paints

puff static bag

heat gun

daisy button

decorative thread

The simple technique of embossing contributes the 'wow factor' to stamping and gives cards a professional, elegant finish. It requires the use of a slow-drying ink, which stays wet long enough to apply embossing powder to the stamped area.

Embossing powders come in a great range of colours. Here, the gold variety – the most popular and a must for your stamping kit – has been used, giving a wonderfully burnished metallic look to the image. Silver embossing powder is also very effective and ideal for celebratory themes (see the Silver Wedding design on page 91).

1 Wipe the surface of the white card with a puff static bag to help prevent unwanted specks of embossing powder clinging to it.

2 Apply the clear embossing ink pad all over the pansy stamp in a dabbing fashion.

3 Firmly stamp the image centrally onto the white card. Hold the card firmly as you carefully lift off the stamp.

4 While the image is still wet, sprinkle gold embossing powder onto it. Tap off the excess powder, then use a paintbrush to dust off any last unwanted specks.

TIP

When you are using the heat gun, make sure that you are working on a heat-protective surface

5 Direct a heat gun at the stamped image and move it back and forth evenly over the design until the image is raised and shiny.

6 Colour in the image with paints, mixing and blending the colours.

The rose image was embossed with gold powder, coloured with brush markers, then cut out and mounted onto torn sage green suede paper. The work was then mounted onto a leaf-stamped purple card.

To finish…
Using double-sided tape, mount the stamped card to the left of the purple card, then mount the paper triangle to butt up centrally against the white card. Mount onto the green card blank. Glue the button to the triangle top and wind round decorative thread.

Gold Embossed Pansy **53**

Embossed Love Letter

This antique postcard design, adorned with hearts and postmarked 14 February, will make a memorable message to someone special on Valentine's Day. For other occasions, just to show a family member or friend that you care, punch out a heart and mount over the postmark with a 3-D foam pad. This project is very like concocting a dish – adding different colours of embossing powder, sprinkling a little here and there, then cooking up the mixture. The pearlized powders used bring a rich quality to the work.

You will need...

cream card
9x11cm (3½x4½in)

cream card blank
13cm (5½in) square

wine suede card
10x12.5cm (4x5in),
plus extra for hearts

scraps of cream suede card

handwritten postcard stamp

black pigment ink pad

pearlized embossing
powder: rose quartz,
amethyst, ruby and
champagne pearl

heat gun

heart punch

1 Ink the postcard stamp with the black pigment ink pad, pressing it down firmly to ensure that all the rubber is covered.

2 Firmly press the stamp centrally onto the cream card, taking care not to rock the stamp. Carefully lift off the stamp, holding the card firmly with your other hand.

3 Spoon different-coloured embossing powders onto the stamped image – rose quartz on the top left-hand and bottom right-hand hearts; amethyst on the postmark and stamp; ruby and amethyst on the dots and parallel lines; champagne pearl on the main script.

4 Tap the excess embossing powder into a container and store – the powder can be used again in other stamping projects.

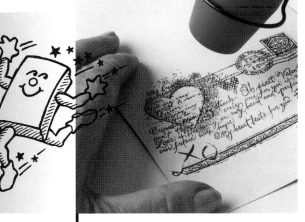

TIP
Make your own postmark by cutting out and mounting a card circle with the date you are sending the card or a birthday date.

5 Dust off any unwanted specks of powder with a paintbrush. Direct a heat gun at the image and move it back and forth evenly across the design until the image is raised and shiny. Do not overheat the powder or it will dull.

6 Using double-sided tape, mount the work centrally onto the wine suede card, then mount onto the cream card blank.

This violet design was stamped with a clear embossing pad, then the violets, writing and border sprinkled with tanzanite Pearlustre™ embossing powder and the leaves with Pearlustre™ aventurine. The violet centres were highlighted with yellow Liquid Pearls™.

To finish…
Punch out hearts from wine and cream suede card. Enclose the hearts in your card, so that when the recipient opens it, they will flutter out!

Embossed Love Letter **55**

Double Embossed Daisies

You will need:

- lilac striped paper
  8.5x14cm (3½x5½in)
- purple card
  9.5x14.5cm (3¾x5¾in)
- lavender card blank
  16x11cm (6¼x4½in),
  used horizontally
- row of flowers, butterfly
  and bug stamp
- black pigment ink pad
- clear embossing powder
- dual embossing pens: shades
  of purple, lilac and red
- heat gun
- 2x⅛in purple eyelets
- ⅛in eyelet holepunch
  and fixing tool
- craft hammer
- 1.5cm (⅝in) wide purple
  sheer ribbon

Purple shadows, a garden of delights and mystical words set the mood for this double embossing project.

With this technique, the outline of the stamp is embossed, then the image coloured, sprinkled with clear embossing powder and heated. Special embossing pens can be used for colouring, which stay wetter longer, or the images can be coloured with ordinary felt-tip pens or coloured pencils and painted with embossing fluid. Then the designs are again sprinkled with clear embossing powder and heated. This technique produces a shiny, enamel-like finish.

1 Ink the stamp all over with a black pigment ink pad using a dabbing action.

2 Firmly stamp centrally onto the striped paper. Carefully lift off the stamp, holding the paper.

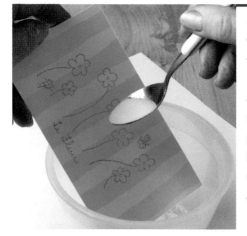

3 Sprinkle clear embossing powder over the wet image and tap off any excess powder. Use a paintbrush to brush off any unwanted specks of powder.

4 Direct a heat gun at the image and move it back and forth evenly across the design until the image is raised and shiny.

TIP
If the paper is absorbent, colour in only some of the images at a time and emboss in case the ink dries out.

5 Use dual embossing pens to colour in the daisy heads, alternating the colours, and finish by carefully colouring in the butterfly and bug.

6 Sprinkle clear embossing powder over the coloured images, tapping off the excess powder. Emboss using a heat gun as in Step 4.

Santa's hat was stamped and double-embossed as in the daisy design but coloured with a crimson dual embossing pen. Crystal glitter glue was applied to the white fur, and the panel was framed with glued-on cord.

7 Mount the work centrally onto purple card, then mount onto the lavender card blank, close to the bottom edge. Insert a pair of purple eyelets through the top centre of the card front (see page 49), thread through ribbon and tie the ends in a bow.

Gold-on-Suede Poinsettia

You will need:

rich crimson suede card and
    card blank 12.5cm (5in) square

sheet of gold mirror card

poinsettia stamp

clear embossing pad

gold glitter embossing powder

heat gun

gold ribbon

Suede is a luxuriously plush medium for stamping, and gives an opulent, highly sophisticated result. Fortunately, the technique is much easier in practice than it looks.

It is now possible to purchase pre-cut suede card blanks and standard-sized sheets of suede card from craft shops and suppliers in a wonderfully rich range of colours.

Try stamping onto white suede and colouring the images with coloured pencils, or use fabric pens or fabric ink pads applied with a paintbrush. Have fun experimenting!

1 Ink the stamp all over with a very wet clear embossing pad using a dabbing action – suede is very absorbent, so it is important for the ink pad to be sufficiently wet.

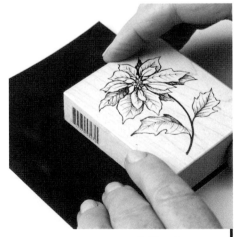

2 Firmly stamp onto the suede card. Carefully lift off the stamp, holding the card.

3 Immediately sprinkle the gold glitter embossing powder over the stamped image (the card will absorb the ink fast), then gently tap off the excess powder. Dust off any unwanted specks of powder with a paintbrush.

4 Direct a heat gun at the image first from the underside of the card (to prevent the powder being blown across the card as it melts). Then bring the heat gun round to the front and move it back and forth evenly until the image is raised and shiny. It is difficult to tell with glitter embossing powders when they have become embossed, so let it cool, then test it with your finger to see if it has melted. Overheating will result in the powder disappearing into the suede.

TIP
Glitter embossing powder, which is less finely ground than other embossing powders, works best on fabric as it does not migrate so easily into the fabric fibres.

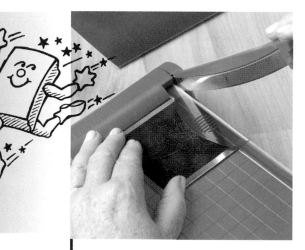

5 Trim the suede card to 7.5 × 6.5cm (3 × 2½in), then mount with double-sided tape onto gold card. Trim the gold card to 9 × 7.5cm (3½ × 3in).

A wedding-dress stamp was inked with embossing ink and stamped onto peach suede paper. The image was sprinkled with pearlized carnelian embossing powder and heat embossed. Cream card was adhered to peach card, then peach silk mulberry paper and striped fabric collaged on top. Finally the dress, ribbon and heart charms were added.

6 Attach a length of gold ribbon centred horizontally around the crimson suede card blank, then mount the stamped panel centrally onto the card using double-sided tape.

Multi-Metallic Angel

You will need…

royal blue card blank
13cm (5in) square

angel stamp

black pigment ink pad

clear embossing powder

heat-resistant acetate
13x11cm (5x4¼in)

multicoloured metal leaf

heat gun

plastic tray

rough sponge

six square gold eyelets

⅛in eyelet holepunch and
fixing tool

craft hammer

self-adhesive notes

This stylized angel image is reminiscent of a stained-glass window design, so it makes the ideal subject for the inventive decorative treatment it is given here. The angel is first stamped onto acetate, to create a glass-like effect, and then embellished with multicoloured metal leaf, which gives the impression of sunlight shining through a church window. The metal leaf is available, inexpensively, in bags of loose pieces of different-coloured leaf, and is applied to the acetate with spray adhesive.

Let this divine project be the inspiration for you to experiment with metal leaf in other stamping designs.

1 Ink the stamp all over with a black pigment ink pad using a dabbing action. Firmly stamp centrally onto the acetate. Carefully lift off the stamp, holding the acetate.

2 Sprinkle clear embossing powder over the wet image and tap off the excess powder. Direct a heat gun at the image and move it back and forth evenly across the design until the image is raised and shiny.

3 Turn over the stamped acetate and spray evenly with spray adhesive over the angel image (spray outdoors in a box to avoid breathing in the fumes).

4 Working in a large tray, to avoid undue mess, select different-coloured pieces of metal leaf to decorate the angel.

5 Press firmly down onto the pieces of metal leaf, covering all the sticky areas of the acetate.

6 Scrub away the excess metal leaf with a rough sponge, then dust off any loose bits with a large paintbrush.

7 Position the acetate right side up on the card blank, aligning with the right-hand edge. Insert two rows of three eyelets down each side of the acetate (see page 49).

TIP

Be careful when stamping on acetate, as the image can easily blur. If this occurs, wash off, dry with kitchen paper and try again.

8 Mask off the whole of the card with self-adhesive notes, leaving a 5mm (¼in) strip exposed along the fold. Spray with spray adhesive, then apply metal leaf to the strip as in Steps 5 and 6. Remove the notes to reveal a metal leaf border.

Polymer Clay Peace Dove

pearlized brushed pewter card
blank 14cm (5½in) square

natural corrugated card
4x9cm (1½x3½in)

transparent dove stamp and
acrylic block

small decorative script stamp

madonna blue inkcredible™
ink pad

pearlescent gold or copper
and crimson brilliance™
ink pads

veggie leather™ (available
from craft shops)

polymer clay: ecru

heat gun

rolling pin

sponge

metallic fabric

gold-edged ribbon in two
contrasting colours

sticky fixes

Polymer clay is a fun, easy-to-work-with medium which offers an exciting array of creative possibilities for your stamped cards. It can be used in the form of a decorative disc, as in this project, or made into a badge or brooch and pinned to the front of a card as a unique way to present a gift.

Alternatively, mould the clay into decorative beads for threading onto cords or tassels for adorning bookmarks or cards. Or why not try creating your own novelty shaped and stamped fridge magnets, gluing a magnet to the reverse of the finished art pieces.

I With the dove stamp nearby, heat the Veggie Leather™ with a heat gun until it starts smoking. Quickly stamp the dove stamp onto the Veggie Leather before it cools.

2 Soften the polymer clay with your hands, then roll out with a rolling pin over the impression left in the Veggie Leather™.

3 Lift off the clay – you should have a clear raised dove image on the clay. Trim the clay to the shape required with a craft knife.

4 Stamp the script stamp onto the clay around the dove, being careful to avoid the touching the dove image. At this point, the script will be fairly indistinct.

6 Direct a heat gun at the inked clay – you will notice that the ink brings out the lettering. Bake the clay in the oven following the manufacturer's instructions.

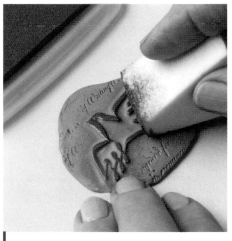

5 Colour the clay with the madonna blue Inkcredible™ ink pad. If the colour is too vibrant, you can wash a little of it away in water – this ink is only set after heating.

7 Remove the clay from the oven and allow to cool. Sponge the dove with ink from the gold or copper ink pad.

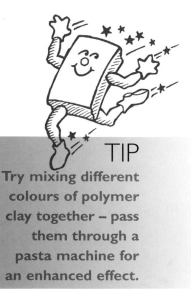

TIP

Try mixing different colours of polymer clay together – pass them through a pasta machine for an enhanced effect.

8 Colour the tops of the ridges of the corrugated card by rubbing with the crimson ink pad.

To finish…

Attach a square of metallic fabric diagonally to the pewter card blank with spray adhesive. Arrange and attach two lengths of contrasting ribbon, then corrugated card on top with double-sided tape. Position the clay disc centrally with sticky fixes.

Scenic Art

soft green card
10x11cm (4x4¼in)

terracotta card
10.5x11.5cm (4¼x4½in)

natural corrugated card
13x4cm (5¼x1½in)

moss green card blank
13cm (5¼in) square

mauve and green
mottled paper

stamps: mallard duck and
reeds, winter trees
and crackle

black pigment ink pad

permanent fine-tip pen

crystal glitter glue

punches: fish and
fishing rod

silver thread

¹⁄₁₆in holepunch

medium copper wire

twig

There are relatively few male-orientated stamping designs for cards, but here an appealing action-packed country scene has been conjured up by an inventive combination of images and the judicious use of coloured paper.

Perspective has been created by adding a line of trees towards the top of the card to form a horizon. The fish in the foreground are then positioned in such a way as to create the impression of movement, leaping in and out of the water.

Why not round the design off with a teasing greeting – 'To the best catch of the day'!

1 Ink the duck stamp all over with a black pigment ink pad using a dabbing action. Firmly stamp onto the soft green card. Carefully lift off the stamp, holding the card.

2 Working over scrap paper, ink the winter trees stamp with the black pigment ink pad, then stamp along the top of the card, either side of the duck (it does not matter if you stamp across the duck).

3 If one of the stamped images has not come out completely, touch it up with a black permanent fine-tip pen.

4 Ink the duck stamp with the black pigment ink and stamp only the duck portion of the stamp onto the mauve and green mottled paper. Lift the stamp off carefully.

TIP

If you cannot find a suitable mottled paper, sponge ink directly from ink pads onto paper, overlapping the colours to create the desired effect.

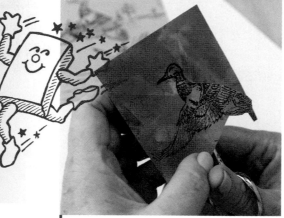

5 Carefully cut out the duck image, keeping any paper offcuts for punching out the fish.

6 Glue the duck cutout directly over the stamped duck image.

7 Punch out three fish from the mottled paper. Ink the crackle stamp with black pigment ink and stamp across the fish to give the effect of scales. Glue two fish to the left of the reeds, referring to the finished card as a guide to positioning. Apply crystal glitter glue to the fish to give a glistening wet appearance.

To finish…

Assemble and glue together the background cards and the stamped card, referring to the finished card as a guide. Punch out and glue the fishing rod in place. Glue a silver thread between the end of the rod and one of the fish. Punch an eye in the third fish, thread through copper wire and wind around a twig. Attach the twig down the left-hand side of the card with double-sided tape.

Antique Heirloom Collage

white card 14x21cm (5½x8¼in)

two rectangles of cream card
14x21cm (5½x8¼in)

sheet of floral-patterned
tissue paper

embedded 'nature' paper
14x21cm (5½x8¼in)

black suede paper
14x13cm (5½x5¼in)

three sisters period
portrait stamp

leaf and button sewing stamp

tape measure and
button stamp

shipping script stamp

black brilliance™ ink pad

brush markers: purple,
blue, green and flesh

tea bag

antique black lace

2 small magnolia leaves

2 mother-of-pearl buttons

black chenille cord

crystal beads

Collage is an art form in itself – assembling and arranging assorted images into a harmonious and pleasing composition. This is the ideal opportunity for collecting and collating unusual stamping designs and combining them with decorative materials to contribute depth, texture and colour to your work, to create a unique piece of art.

Collage is also a great way of preserving memories. For example, you could incorporate theatre tickets, old banknotes, labels, leaves, beads and fabric trimmings into your designs. So start searching for those creative possibilities now!

Two sets of lettering stamps were used here, combined with a subtly coloured lady in an orchard image. Moths, sprigs and assorted perfume labels were then incorporated.

A stamped script was sponged with colour, then a vine leaf was stamped at random and a rose border added. A cutout female image, perfume label and heart charm complete the design.

1 Ink the sisters stamp all over with a black Brilliance™ ink pad, then firmly stamp onto the white card. Stamp the other images, except the script, in the same way.

2 When the sisters image is dry, age the photo area with a damp tea bag or dissolved coffee grains. Colour in the flowers and leaves with brush markers. Cut out the leaf and button image and colour. Cut out a portion of the tape measure image, ending with a button at either end.

3 Ink the script stamp with the Brilliance™ ink pad and stamp onto the patterned tissue paper. Repeat underneath to fill the paper – the images need not align.

4 Tear the stamped tissue paper to fit onto the nature paper. Stick the stamped tissue paper to the nature paper with spray adhesive.

5 Glue a length of antique lace vertically towards the right-hand side of the black suede paper, folding any excess to the underside.

6 Glue one piece of cream card to the back of the nature paper to strengthen. Mount the suede paper with lace onto the left-hand side of the nature paper using double-sided tape. Attach the other piece of cream card to the rest of the suede, leaving a 3mm (⅛in) margin between the card pieces as a hinge.

To finish…

Mount all the stamped images and mongolia leaves onto the card with spray adhesive, referring to the finished card. Glue on buttons, tie a length of chenille cord down the card spine, then thread and tie on crystal beads.

Antique Heirloom Collage **67**

Snowflake Windows

This is an inventive way of using the mega punches that are on the market, punching out a series of windows in which snowflakes mounted on circles are strung. But the windows could be used in alternative ways – to frame a message or image stamped on the inside of the card, or photographs of three siblings or an arrangement of pressed flowers. Remember, you could just punch one aperture – or several – and it need not be square. The creative options are infinite!

You will need...

white matt card blank
  20x9.5cm (8x3¾in)

scraps of white and lavender card

snowflake stamp

silver brilliance™ ink pad

self-adhesive note or scrap card

crystal embossing powder

punch for cutting
  3.5cm (1⅜in) squares

punch to cut
  3cm (1¼in) rounds

snowflake punches in
  three designs

heat gun

fine crystal glitter

diamond dots

18cm (7in) purple
  embroidery yarn

snowflake frost a peel

sticky fixes

1 Using the square punch, punch out a vertical row of three evenly spaced squares from the white card blank.

2 Use self-adhesive notes or scrap card to shield the inside of the card behind the apertures. Ink the stamp all over with silver ink. Firmly stamp randomly over the card, then carefully lift off the stamp, holding the card.

3 Sprinkle crystal embossing powder over the wet image and tap off the excess powder. Direct a heat gun at the image and move it back and forth evenly across the design until the image is raised and shiny.

4 Colour the white card with silver ink directly from the ink pad using even strokes.

TIP

Punch down the leading edge of a card and thread through a colourful ribbon for a birthday design, or cream for a wedding.

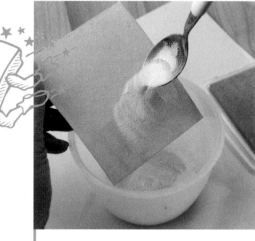

5 Sprinkle crystal embossing powder over the surface of the inked card and tap off the excess. Direct a heat gun over the surface to emboss. When cool, punch out two circles and two snowflakes from the silver card. Punch out four circles and one snowflake from lavender card.

6 Spray one side of the four lavender circles with spray adhesive and sprinkle with glitter. Repeat with the silver side of one silver circle.

7 Glue the two silver snowflakes to the two glitter-coated lavender circles and a lavender snowflake to the glitter-coated silver circle. Use a craft knife to pick up Diamond Dots and place in the centres of the punched and stamped snowflakes.

8 Attach yarn top and bottom inside the card with a Snowflake Frost A Peel. Using sticky fixes, sandwich the thread between one decorated (facing outwards) and one plain lavender circle at the top aperture. Repeat with silver circles at the middle, then lavender at the bottom. Place a Snowflake Frost A Peel above and below the middle aperture to secure the yarn. Decorate the inside circles with Snowflake Frost A Peels.

Mounting Magic

There is an endless variety of beautiful coloured card and textured, metallic and corrugated papers available to set off and add dimension to your stamped artwork. Tearing paper gives an attractive handmade look to a card – brush the edges of mulberry with a wet paintbrush and allow the water to soak in before gently tearing.

Establish in advance if you need to trim down the stamped card before you mount it and if it can be layered several times before the final mounting. Be sure to coordinate colours and check for balance in the width of borders. Remember that less is more.

You will need...

dark pink plain paper 6x9cm (2½x3½in)

pink floral paper 9.5cm (3¾in) square, plus extra for daisies

two squares of pale pink card, 7.5cm (3in) and 8cm (3¼in), plus extra for daisies

wine card blank 13cm (5in) square

open daisy pattern stamp

solid daisy pattern stamp

white pearlescent brilliance™ ink pad

versamark™ resist-ink pad

rose quartz embossing powder

¹⁄₁₆in holepunch

heat gun

daisy pointed petal punch

daisy rounded petal punch

medium or thick silver wire

sticky fixes

pink tissue paper

3-D foam pads

glue pen

1 Trace the carrier-bag template on page 73 onto the back of the dark pink paper and cut out.

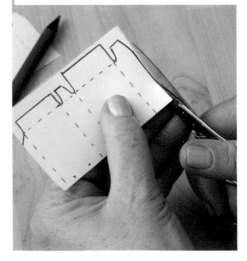

2 Punch out the holes for the handles.

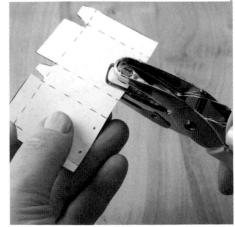

3 Ink the open daisy stamp all over with the white pearlescent ink pad using a dabbing action.

4 Firmly stamp onto the carrier bag. Carefully lift off the stamp, holding the paper.

TIP

When folding paper or card, lay a clean piece of scrap paper over the top as you do it to prevent finger marks spoiling the card.

5 Sprinkle rose quartz embossing powder over the wet image and tap off the excess.

6 Direct a heat gun at the image and move it back and forth evenly across the design until the image is raised and shiny. Assemble the carrier bag following the instructions on page 73.

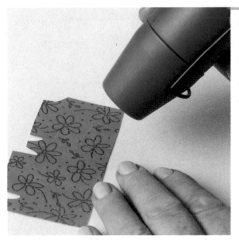

7 Ink the solid daisy stamp all over with the VersaMark™ resist-ink pad using a dabbing action. Firmly stamp onto the slightly smaller pale pink card square. Clean the stamp.

8 Attach the solid daisy-stamped card to the slightly larger pale pink card square, then mount diagonally onto the floral paper with double-sided tape. Mount the work centrally onto the wine card blank.

9 Punch out 18 daisies from the spare pink card and 18 from floral paper using two types of daisy punches. Cut nine 6cm (2½in) lengths of wire for stems. Sandwich the wires between two matching daisy heads using sticky fixes. Shape the wires into curvy stems.

10 Attach the carrier bag to the assembled card with double-sided tape. Add scrunched tissue paper to protrude from the bag. Arrange the flowers on stems in the bag. Mount the daisy heads on the card using 3-D foam pads.

A carrier bag was made from giftwrap, using the template and method opposite. A stocking and message tag were punched from Ultrathin™ shrink plastic, coloured, a hole punched for hanging, then shrunk and attached to the bag along with a sticker mouse.

A Brilliance™ black pad was used to ink the dress stamp, which was stamped onto vellum. When dry, the image was torn around and adhered to a torn purple background using vellum glue. This was mounted onto stripy background paper, then purple card. Rhinestones, a hanger and ribbon were glued on as embellishment.

TO ASSEMBLE THE CARRIER BAG

1. Score along the dotted lines.

2. Carefully fold forwards along the scored lines.

3. Using a glue pen, glue the tab **A** to the underside of the tab **B**, then glue **C** tab to the upper side of the tab **D**. Glue the tab **D** to the underside of the tab **B** and tab **C** over tab **B**.

4. Thread the ends of a length of wire through the holes on each side of the bag and bend back to secure.

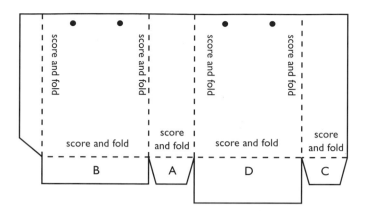

Varying blue and turquoise coloured pencils were blended over smooth matt card, to cover an area 7.5x5cm (3x2in). A dragonfly image was then stamped over this blended area, which in turn was torn around and glued onto card. Glitter glue on the wings completed the design.

Giraffes and leaf fronds were inked with a black pigment ink and stamped onto green matt card. Coloured embossing powder (ochre, terracotta and copper for the giraffes, and ochre, verdigris and emerald for leaves) was carefully sprinkled over wet images and heat embossed. Raffia ribbon was glued to tan base card and the stamped giraffe card glued on top.

Shrink Plastic Heart

cream suede paper
  12cm (4¾in) square

pink net paper 13cm (5in) square

crimson card blank
  13cm (5in) square

hearts and flowers stamp

pearlescent crimson
  brilliance™ ink pad

large pre-cut cream
  shrink plastic heart

talcum powder

small rectangular holepunch

sponge

heat gun

acrylic block (optional)

diamond dots

brooch

sheer ribbon

3-D foam pads

Using shrink plastic is amazing fun, and works on the same principle of the old classic of heating empty crisp packets in the oven until tiny in size. But the safe and successful approach is to use special-purpose shrink plastic, which is available in pre-cut shapes, and a heat gun.

Here, the stamp design on the background paper is echoed in miniature, in all its fine detail, on the heart. You will notice that when the image is shrunk its colour deepens, so if you are looking for a pastel effect, keep colours very light or colour with chalks.

1 Sprinkle talcum powder onto the shrink plastic heart on both sides. This acts as a mild abrasive and helps prevent the plastic from sticking together when shrinking.

2 Ink the stamp all over with the pearlescent crimson Brilliance™ ink pad and carefully stamp centrally onto the heart, taking care to avoid blurring the image. Hold the heart and lift off the stamp. If the image has blurred, wash off the ink and start again.

3 The ink will be wet for some time, so taking care not to smudge the image, punch out rectangular holes in the blank spaces of the heart. Punch a rectangle at the top of the heart for a ribbon.

4 Colour the edge of the heart with the crimson ink using a sponge – again, be careful not to smudge the image.

TIP

If you are interrupted in the shrinking process, the shrink plastic can simply be reheated.

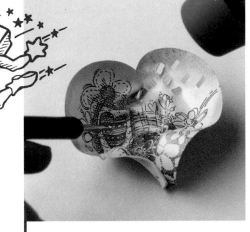

5 Using a tool to hold the heart in place, direct a heat gun at the heart, holding it further away than usual at first. This will help to dry off the ink before it starts shrinking, so that the image does not smudge. Move the heat gun closer.

6 Keep the heat gun directed on the heart, which will curl up but straighten itself with further heating. If the heart does not flatten out, use an acrylic block, while the plastic is still hot, to flatten it.

7 Ink the stamp again using the crimson ink pad but very wet and stamp onto the cream suede paper, pressing down firmly before lifting off while holding the paper. Tear around the heart image. Roughly cut out the net paper slightly larger all round than the torn suede.

8 Mount the net paper onto the crimson card blank, then the stamped suede with double-sided tape. Stick Diamond Dots to the centres of the daisies on the suede and heart. Attach a brooch and thread ribbon through the hole at the top of the heart. Mount onto the card with 3-D foam pads.

Christmas Tree Cutout

Shaped cards always make a great impact and this festive favourite presents the perfect project for all the family to partake in. Children will be fully entertained helping you to dress the tree, involving several different craft techniques. But they will especially love watching the plastic snowmen shrink!

Look for other shaped cards from craft suppliers. Alternatively, make your own denim pocket shape, then anchor it to the base card with eyelets to look like rivets. Banknotes protruding from the pocket would complete a fun idea for giving money as a gift.

You will need...

- christmas tree card
- stamps: fir tree, wire stars border, bauble and snowflake
- forest green and gold pigment ink pads
- black and green brilliance™ ink pads
- crystal embossing powder
- gold glitter embossing powder
- narrow strips of self-adhesive paper: gold, copper and silver
- ultrathin™ shrink plastic
- gold leaf and black permanent pen
- heat gun
- punches: snowman and stocking
- red and green glitter glue
- red and green crystal jewels
- gold ribbon
- sticky fixes

1 Ink the fir tree stamp all over with a forest green pigment ink pad using a dabbing action. Firmly stamp onto the tree card. Carefully lift off the stamp, holding the card. Repeat until the whole tree card is covered, to give it depth. Sprinkle crystal embossing powder over the wet images and tap off the excess.

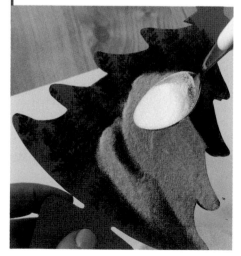

2 Direct a heat gun at the image and move it back and forth evenly across the design until the image is raised and shiny.

3 Ink the wire stars border stamp all over with a gold pigment ink pad using a dabbing action. Firmly stamp onto the tree card to look like a garland. Repeat until you have four garlands.

4 Sprinkle gold glitter embossing powder over all the wet images and tap off the excess. Direct a heat gun back and forth evenly across the design until raised and shiny.

TIP

Ultrathin™ shrink plastic is like a thin plastic paper and is much easier to punch than ordinary shrink plastic.

5 Place evenly spaced paper strips on the tree pot and trim to length. Decorate between them. Colour the star with a gold leaf pen.

6 Ink the bauble stamp with the black Brilliance™ ink pad and carefully stamp onto Ultrathin™ shrink plastic – the surface is slippery and could easily blur the image. Lift off the stamp, holding the plastic. Stamp six baubles. When dry (a few hours), cut out, discarding the ribbon.

7 Punch snowmen and stockings out of the shrink plastic. Draw faces and buttons on the snowmen with a black permanent pen. Stamp the snowflake pattern onto the stockings using green Brilliance™ ink. Heat the shrink plastic pieces with a heat gun, holding them in place with a tool, until they totally reduce in size. They will curl up but straighten out by continuing to heat.

8 Colour the berries on the baubles and tops and toes of the stockings with red glitter glue and the holly leaves with green glitter glue.

To finish…

Attach the shrink plastic ornaments to the card with sticky fixes. Add red and green crystal jewels and tie a gold ribbon around the trunk.

Rose Series

You will need...

white glossy card

forest green card blanks
21x10cm (8¼x4in)

light and dark green
vellum paper

transparent rose stem stamp
and acrylic block

dual embossing pens:
poppy red, spring green
and bottle green

clear embossing powder

dark green pen

heat gun

⅛in holepunch or darning
needle

1.5cm (⅝in) wide red
voile ribbon

netting

Here you will see how to make a batch of this exquisite rose design – perfect for a special-occasion invitation – the surefire way (see Making Multiples, pages 14–15, for further tips).

The embossing is the main potential pitfall. Inking all the cards in one go is not a workable option, since the ink may dry before you have completed embossing the whole batch. So with each card in turn, ink and add the embossing powder, tapping off the excess. Space the cards out to avoid overlapping them and disturbing the embossing powder which is not yet heat set. You can then heat and melt the powder of one card after another.

1 Position the rose stamp on the acrylic block. Colour the rosebuds of the stamp with the red dual embossing pen and the stems and leaves with two shades of green dual embossing pen.

2 Stamp onto the glossy card, pressing on top of the stamp firmly to help blend the green inks. Lift the stamp off, holding the card firmly. Clean the stamp.

3 Sprinkle clear embossing powder over the wet image and tap off the excess. Repeat this process for all the cards in the series.

4 Taking each card in turn, direct a heat gun at the image and move it back and forth evenly across the design, until the image is raised and shiny.

TIP

Tie a label to the bow of each card, and write a message for the recipient.

5 Punch a hole either side of the stem on each card. If your punch cannot reach, use a darning needle.

6 Thread a length of ribbon through the holes on each card.

7 Cut a triangle of netting for each card. Cover the rose stem of each card with a netting triangle, then tie the ribbon in a bow around it, to resemble a bouquet.

To finish…

Tear a strip of light and dark green vellum paper for each card and mount with a little glue, one overlapping the other, a third of the way down each card blank. Mount the rose cards centrally on top with double-sided tape.

TRY THIS

Always be proud of your artwork and sign it! To coordinate with this design, tear a small piece of light and dark green vellum for each card, glue to the back and sign your work with dark green pen.

Artful Embellishments

All kinds of simple decorative elements can give a project a special individuality or add a finishing touch. This is where you can let your creativity run wild. Collect interesting items from junk shops – for instance, items of jewellery that can be broken up, including attractive beads. Check old clothing for pieces of lace or fancy buttons. Old postcards can be photocopied and used as background paper. Remember not to overlook natural materials such as flowers and leaves for pressing, twigs and shells. Glitter and other specialist products like Liquid Pearls™ and Liquid Appliqué™ are also invaluable for adding extra texture and interest.

Woolly Sheep Tag

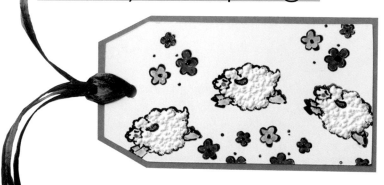

To prepare…

Using the template on page 100, cut out a pink card tag and a slightly smaller white card tag. Position the white tag centrally on the pink and punch out the hole. Emboss the sheep images using a black pigment ink pad and clear embossing powder. Colour the legs grey and the cheeks and ears pink with brush markers.

1 Apply white Liquid Appliqué™ and distribute evenly over the sheep's bodies.

2 Direct a heat gun over the Liquid Appliqué™ and heat until it resembles a woolly coat.

To finish…

Stamp some daisies and colour. Mount the white tag onto the pink tag with double-sided tape. Thread bright raffia through the hole and tie.

The Santa image was embossed with black pigment ink and clear embossing powder, then coloured with a dual embossing pen and embossed again. The Liquid Appliqué™, (hat trim, eyebrows and beard woolly), was sprinkled with crystal glitter when still warm. A tiny bell was then glued to the hat.

Glittered & Gilded Pine

To prepare…

Colour a pine needle and cone stamp with green and brown brush markers and stamp onto white glossy card. Highlight the needles and cones with crystal glitter. Mount onto a copper mirror card blank with double-sided tape. Use the template on page 100, reduced in size, to cut out two small tags. Punch out the holes.

1 Dab the edges of the tags into a copper Brilliance™ ink pad, working your way round until all the sides are gilded.

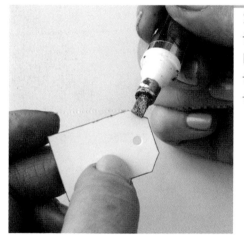

2 Alternatively, run the nib of a gold leaf pen around the edges of the tags to gild.

3 Using round-nosed pliers, thread medium copper wire through each tag and wind around a short twig.

To finish…

Mount on the card with sticky fixes. Write a greeting on the tags, such as 'Happy Christmas'.

This snowdrop was to stamped onto white matt card with green pigment ink, then heat embossed with clear embossing powder. The edges of the card were coloured and embossed in the same way. The design was mounted onto white card, then onto square moss green card. The snowdrop and ground were highlighted with crystal glitter glue for a frost effect.

Wire-Haired Ballerina

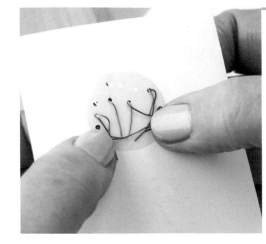

To prepare…

Ink the ballerina stamp with a black permanent ink pad and stamp onto white matt card. Colour in using brush markers.

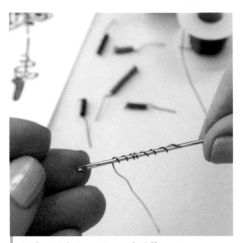

1 Cut 12 lengths of different-coloured medium wire. Twist around a darning needle to form coils. Stick a patch of heavy duty double-sided tape onto the back of the stamped card, positioning it as near as possible to the back of the ballerina's head. Leave the backing on the tape.

2 Using a ⅛in holepunch, punch 12 holes in the ballerina's hair from the front of the card. Remove the backing from the patch of double-sided tape.

3 Push the wire coils through the holes from the front of the card and press the ends of the coils onto the sticky tape at the back.

4 Stick another patch of double-sided tape over the first to hold the wires firmly in place.

To finish…

Mount a purple card background onto a lime green card blank with double-sided tape. Attach a length of ribbon to the left of the card, then mount the ballerina card on top with double-sided tape. Finally, give her a mad hair day by pulling out the wire coils and hooking the ends onto each other.

Pearlized Wedding Attire

To prepare…

Ink the wedding clothes stamp with a black Brilliance™ ink pad and stamp onto swirly-patterned vellum paper and allow to dry.

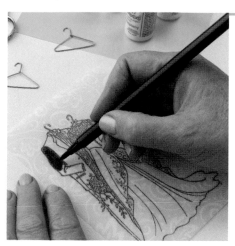

I Working on the reverse side of the stamped image to give a softer look, colour in the morning suit with black brush marker.

2 Distribute small drops of oyster Liquid Pearls™ down the back of the bride's dress to look like pearls.

3 Using a paint-brush, colour in the lace on the dress and flowers in the bouquet with oyster Liquid Pearls™ to give them depth.

To finish…

Attach the vellum to a pearlized lilac card blank by punching two holes with an eyelet punch through the front of the card only and fixing eyelets (see page 49), then threading through and tying sheer ribbon. Decorate miniature wire coathangers with ribbon to match and attach to the card with strong glue.

For an alternative luxurious embellishing approach, self-adhesive crystal jewels were used to decorate a butterfly image, which was stamped with black pigment ink, clear embossed and coloured in with brush markers.

21st Birthday

The keys were stamped out in permanent black dye-based ink onto a torn script background, sponged yellow and green. This was then mounted onto a deckle-edged background. The keys were highlighted with silver pen and glitter glue. A great card for 'Coming of Age' or 'Moving Home'.

Birthday & Friendship

Best Friends

The 'friend' stamp was inked with embossing ink, stamped onto a co-ordinating background paper, and embossed with white embossing powder. This was mounted with eyelets onto torn russet paper, and this mounted onto white card with background paper adhered. To finish, two white butterfly peel-offs were mounted onto background paper, cut out and 3D'd to the card. Further white daisy peel-offs were used as highlights.

Daisy Tag Art

Three different daisies were stamped onto tags (template on page 100) with black pigment ink, clear embossed and coloured with brush markers. Green torn vellum was stamped with tiny leaves using moss green ink and clear embossed. The punched holes were covered with eyelet peel-offs and threaded with decorative thread.

Sunflower Square

The sunflower was stamped with black pigment ink onto green vellum and clear embossed. The cutout image was brayered on the reverse with aurora Brilliance™ ink, backed with white card and 3-D mounted onto white card decorated with torn strips of vellum.

Daisy Trio

A square shadow stamp was stamped onto gloss card with dye-based purple, apricot and raspberry ink, sprayed lightly with water to give a watercolour effect. Daisies were stamped with pigment ink and clear embossed. A purple ribbon was glued to the base card. 'Happy Birthday' or 'Thank You' could be added either side.

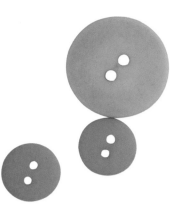

Sail Away

Two pieces of watercolour card and base card were sponged with sea and pale blue dye-based ink. A lighthouse was stamped on one card piece (and base card edge), torn out and mounted; a boat peel-off attached to the other, cut out and 3-D mounted. Torn blue vellum, seagull peel-offs and tiny gold beads were added.

Cards For Men

Beach Comber

Shells were stamped onto white card using a blue dye-based ink, the edge lightly sponged. Shells and dots were highlighted with brush marker and glitter glue applied to the large dots. The card was fixed to dark blue card with paper fasteners (brats). The background was stamped with a crackle-effect texture cube. A bow and shell complete the design.

Bird Watching

The bird and birdhouse was stamped onto gloss card and coloured with brush markers – greens and browns for the leaves, black and brown for the birdhouse and black and blue for the birds. It was mounted onto three-toned background paper and a blue base card. This card could also be used for Easter.

Gold Leaf

Magnolia leaves were stamped onto burgundy card with a VersaMark™ ink pad and Pearl Ex™ pigment powder in different colours was applied with a paintbrush. The card was trimmed with deckle-edged scissors, the edge highlighted with a gold leaf pen and 3-D-mounted onto gold card.

Embossed Ferns

A wide strip was trimmed from either end of the card front to leave a central flap, which can be lifted to reveal a stamped message. The card was sponged all over with yellow, green, orange and deep peach Brilliance™ inks. The stamped fern image on the flap and the sprigs down the sides were gold embossed.

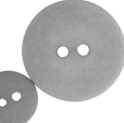

Mosaic Foliage

A sheet of self-adhesive mosaics was sponged with beige to rust colours, then different leaf stamps stamped at random. One tile at a time was then peeled off the backing and evenly spaced onto a black base card.

Dancing Roses

The rose border was stamped onto a dusky pink base card and the row of roses stamped onto white card using crimson Brilliance™ ink, then coloured with soft and dusty pink brush markers. Torn pale pink vellum decorates both cards. A tag could be glued to a rose, carrying a message such as 'Get Well Soon'.

Oriental Poppy

The poppy and Chinese characters were stamped onto a watermark paper (edged with a gold leaf pen) using black permanent ink, then coloured with brush markers and mounted onto a wine base card. A strip of oriental paper, folded lengthways, was attached front and back down the card spine and a bead and tassel added. A suitably sumptuous card to mark a special achievement or event.

Flowerpot Tag

The transparency of the flowerpot, stem, daisy and small tag stamps used here allowed them to be applied separately, and accurately aligned, onto a pre-cut shrink plastic tag. The tag was then shrunk and wire threaded through and curled before being glued to white card, to create a playful design to raise the spirits.

Dynamic Daisy

The daisy was stamped onto a printed watercolour paper using black pigment ink and clear embossed, then highlighted with Dimensional Magic™. Holes punched in the striped background paper and white base card were covered front and back with peel-off eyelets. 'Congratulations' could be stamped across a corner.

Home-Sweet-Home

This adobe house was stamped onto shrink plastic with black Brilliance™ ink, coloured in and cut out. Once shrunk, it was glued onto tan card, then mounted onto russet card. A tan strip decorated with fancy threads embellishes the oatmeal base card.

Moving House

The brushed gold base card was stamped with a leaf scroll and gold embossed all over. The house was cut from cream pearlized card (template on page 100), stamped with a leafy branch design and gold embossed. A punched card circle was decorated with a Class A Peel and 3-D mounted with a tassel.

Sweetheart

This image was stamped onto white card with permanent black dye-based ink. Coloured pencils were used to subtly colour in the flower, mice and ground. A tag was attached with an eyelet, then punched hearts were glued on, showering off the daisy.

Love & Romance

Dragonfly Romance

The design was stamped with a VersaMark™ ink pad, then dusted with decorating chalks to create a soft pastel effect. Torn green vellum was used to decorate the base card and a dragonfly sticker was added to give a three-dimensional effect.

Crystal Snowdrop Tag

This delicate snowdrop was stamped onto the tag using green Brilliance™ ink, then highlighted with crystal glitter glue. Coiled wire and iridescent ribbon were then threaded through the tag. A card could be made to match this gift tag.

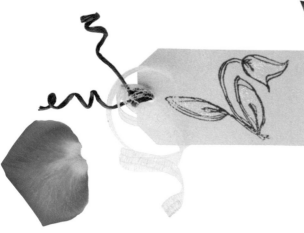

Vintage Wine Tag

The grape image was stamped onto cream card (edged with gold leaf pen) and coloured in with brush markers, then mounted onto torn mulberry paper. The base tag was decorated with glued-on ribbon and threaded with a coordinating ribbon, long enough to tie round a wine bottle.

Opulent Lilies

Lilies were stamped onto a base card using a purple brush marker (only part of the stamp was used), then coloured in with dusky lilac and green brush markers. A coordinating ribbon was tied in place to add a finishing touch.

Silver Wedding

This card was embossed with silver embossing powder for a silver wedding theme. The cats' noses were punched out and diamond-like beads, threaded with silver glitter thread for whiskers, were glued in place. Silver hearts were punched out and randomly glued to the card.

Heart-to-Heart Tag

Two card hearts were cut out and stamped with a scroll stamp using a clear embossing pad, then gold embossed. They were overlapped and a hole punched through both, which was then threaded with ribbon and tied in a bow to create a double tag.

Baby Girl

The image was stamped using a permanent dye-based ink, then coloured in with watercolour pencils and highlighted with crystal glitter glue. The finished design was mounted with two heart eyelets. A safety pin stamp was used on the white base card.

New Baby

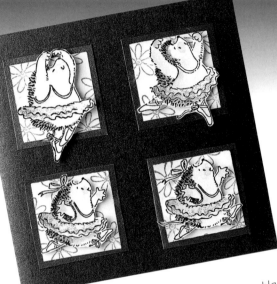

Dancing with Joy

The hedgehogs were stamped with permanent black ink, subtly coloured in with pencils and frills highlighted with crystal glitter glue. Four square tiles were cut from a daisy-stamped background, then mounted onto contrasting tiles and the plum base card. This would make a lovely child's birthday invitation.

Baby Boy

The cutout jumpsuit was stamped with blue Brilliance™ ink. Scallop scissors were used to cut out a square of background, stamped with small daisies using resist ink and blue-ink sponged. The card was assembled using eyelets and the scallops highlighted with Liquid Pearls™.

Bouncing Bunny

Peel-off daisies were used to decorate the bunny, which was stamped with bright pink dye-based ink, and background. A button peel-off, sewn with thread for an authentic look, was positioned in the corners of the base card. A delightful design for a christening.

Baby's World

These images were stamped onto soft multi-coloured brayered card and cut into squares, then tucked into punched photo frame slots in white card squares. The background was enhanced with sheer ribbon and silver dots and the pram with a silver heart. This would make a great first birthday card.

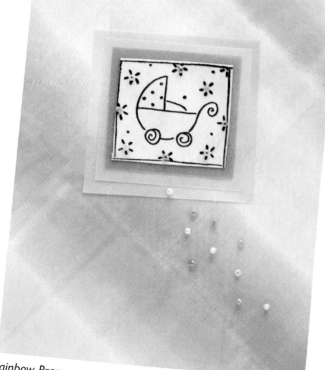

Rainbow Pram

Soft rainbow colours from a multicoloured dye-based ink pad, brayered onto gloss card, enhance this adorable baby design. A piece of white card was brayered with the same colours, stamped with the pram image using permanent ink and mounted onto staggered layers of vellum. Seed beads add dainty highlights.

Musical Union

The rose was gold embossed onto cream card and coloured in with brush markers. The card was aged with sponged green-grey ink, then edged with a gold leaf pen. For the backgrounds, a music score was stamped onto cream card using gold Brilliance™ ink and green card was stamped with a gold scroll design, edged with gold leaf pen.

Wedding

Single Stem Rose

The rose and leaf sprigs were stamped with a clear embossing pad and white embossed, to act as a resist. The card was then brayered with soft beige ink. Beige vellum was torn in a heart shape to frame the rose. This design also looks beautiful simply white embossed on cream.

Wedding Bells

The bell design was gold embossed onto pearly swirled card and highlighted with Diamond Dots. Gold and silver speckled vellum was torn to fit the base card and anchored with tied white and coffee ribbons. Punch tiny hearts to put inside the card.

Floral Celebration

The blossom and script image was stamped onto white card and gold embossed. The part showing was coloured with brush markers. The image was also embossed onto cream card, coloured and cut outs minus the trailing part. The card was assembled as shown, then finished with gold cord and ribbon, leaving trailing ends to echo the image.

Scrolled Heart

An invitation is slotted into a stuck-down vellum envelope with one end cut open, to make a pocket. To enable the card to be easily removed, a semicircle was punched in the vellum using a circle punch. The heart on the invitation was stamped with beige ink and a cream bow tied through two punched holes. Hearts adorn the envelope.

Heart Trio

These beautiful hearts were punched from striped vellum stamped with a rose design using a deep pink pigment ink and clear embossing powder. A strip of stamped vellum was cut for a background. The tags were mounted with 3-D foam pads, threaded with ribbon and the pink hearts decorated with silver hearts.

Trim the Tree

White card was stamped with Christmas trees using permanent black ink, highlighted with green brush marker and gold glitter glue. Red card, with a gold-embossed border, was folded envelope-style around the white card. A blank card square was added for a greeting. Gold cord encloses the card, tying in a tree-stamped shrink plastic decoration.

Christmas

Christmas Carol

This design was gold embossed onto cream vellum and the squares coloured with red and green brush markers. The green base card was embellished with a gold-embossed spiral border design. Torn sheet music and vellum were used as layered backgrounds.

Three Wise Men

Stars were stamped at random in silver ink on royal blue card. A gloss card was sprayed lightly with water and brayered with blue and purple inks from a multicoloured pad. A 'peace on earth' design was stamped with black pigment ink and clear embossed. A corner punch was used to decorate the layered frames.

Waiting for Santa

Liquid Appliqué™ was applied to the middle stocking top of three stockings punched from striped metallic foil. Pegs were glued to a line of gold-embossed pinecone sprigs. Gold snowflakes, amber jewels and gold ribbon provide the finishing touches. A message tag could also be pegged up with family names or Christmas wishes.

Penguin Trio

In this 3-D découpage design, the bodies of the stamped, coloured and cut-out penguins were 3-D'd twice and Santa's hat three times. The punched snowflakes were high-lighted with glitter and attached randomly to the background. The card was then mounted onto white card, then turquoise suede card.

Snow Frolics

A great design for a child's Christmas party invitation. The children were stamped with dark blue permanent ink onto white card, coloured in using watercolour pencils and highlighted with 'frosty' crystal glitter glue. The snowflake-stamped base card was decorated with uneven shapes.

Easter Rose

Stamped and embossed in gold, the rose image was then coloured in using brush markers, mounted onto gold sparkly paper, then onto cream cracked-leather-look card. A yellow ribbon was added and a tag cut from the leather-look card attached to carry a message – 'Happy Easter' or 'Spring is in the Air'.

Spring has Sprung

The crocus image was stamped three times using black permanent ink and coloured in using brush markers. The stamped card was then torn along the bottom edge and mounted onto similarly torn plum corrugated card. The sheer ribbon contributes a little drama.

Easter Eggs

These Easter eggs were stamped with multicoloured pigment ink onto gloss card and clear embossed. They were then cut out and mounted using 3-D foam pads onto checked ribbon, adhered to a lime green background and attached to a purple card. Sticker daisies add a final colourful touch.

Lady Liberty

This Lady Liberty image was stamped using permanent black ink and coloured in with pencils – blue around the stars and red stripes; golden orange blended with yellow for the hair. To keep on the patriotic theme for July 4th, it was mounted onto red and blue cards, then finished with a brass star.

Halloween Pumpkin

The image was stamped onto white card using black pigment ink and clear embossed, then mounted onto orange and then black card. Stars and swirls were stamped at random and gold-embossed. 'It's a party' could also be stamped onto the card.

Fallen Fall Leaves

The leaves, from a transparent stamp set, were stamped using multicoloured dye-based ink – seeing through the stamps and blocks allows you to place them accurately. Leaves were punched out in lavender and purple card, gently rubbed across the ink pad and 3-D mounted. An unexpected colour scheme!

Cat-in-the-Hat

This fun Halloween design was stamped using black pigment ink, clear embossed and coloured in with brush markers, with a few star stickers added. Glitter glue was applied to the hat and pumpkin. A funky yellow sticker border frames the image.

Templates

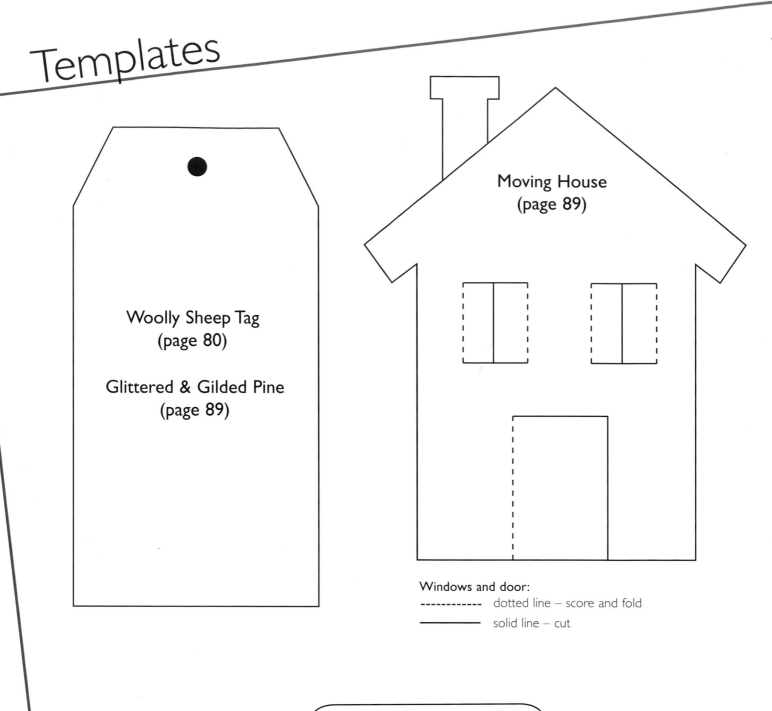

Woolly Sheep Tag
(page 80)

Glittered & Gilded Pine
(page 89)

Moving House
(page 89)

Windows and door:

- - - - - - - - - - - -   dotted line – score and fold

——————   solid line – cut

Creative Craft Combo
(pages 50–51)

Daisy Tag Art
(page 85)

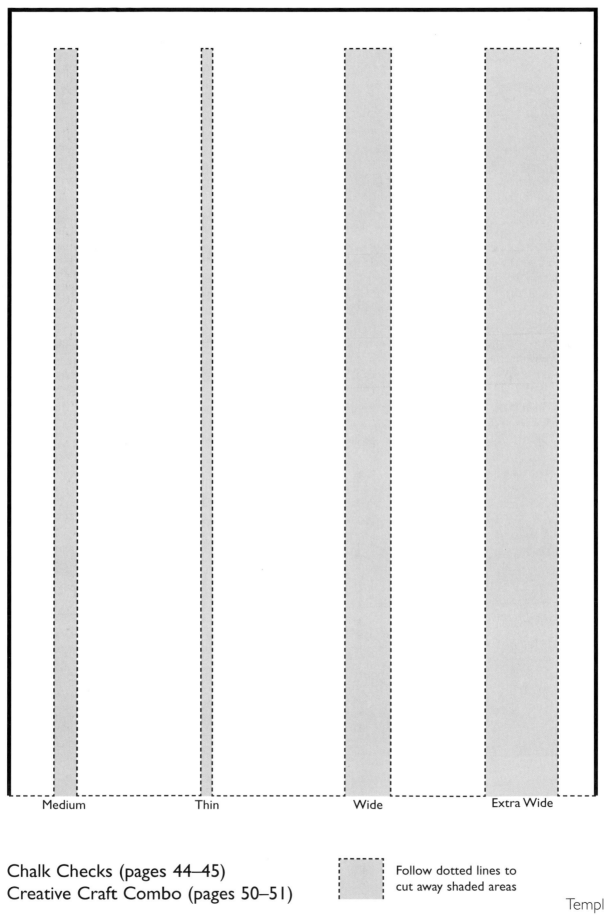

Medium   Thin   Wide   Extra Wide

Chalk Checks (pages 44–45)
Creative Craft Combo (pages 50–51)

Follow dotted lines to
cut away shaded areas

Product Details

To follow are details of the products used in the main projects. Please refer to the Suppliers and Retailers for contact details.

Brush Marker Blooms (p16)
• Lasting Impressions green dotted card • Stamp: Magenta 23.520.0 • Marvy brush markers: leaf green and purple

Tonal Leaves (p18)
• Stamp: Magenta 28007.1
• Marvy brush markers: orange, red, yellow ochre and olive green

Shadow-Blended Stem (p20)
• Stamps: Rubber Stampede 3 Squares foam block shadow stamp; Stemmed Floral foam block stamp

Pencil Blended Bookmark (p22)
• Stamp: Stampendous Maggie's Flower Set

Water-Brushed Framed Flower (p24)
• Stamp: Magenta 23.585.5
• Magenta Memories paper heart border sticker

Sponged Butterfly Backdrop (p26)
• Stamps: Penny Black 1807E Butterfly; Hero Arts A2148 Spiral Flower Pop

Spiral Daisy Photo Frame (p28)
• Stamp: Magenta 14315.0 Daisy

Multi-Inked Maple Leaves (p30)
• Stamps: Stampendous Q089 Large Maple Points; Stampendous D102 Small Maple Points; Annette Allen Watkins D1101 Dotted Line
• Vivid™ multicoloured dye-based ink pad: Indian Summer

Fancy Frames (p32)
• Craftwork Cards gift token card 21×10cm (8¼x4in)
• Stamp: Stampendous CCP001 Garden Sampler
• Vivid™ multicoloured dye-based ink pad: Dynamic

Bleached Sunflower Label (p34)
• Stamps: Stamp Studio Sunflower Tag; Stampendous XXA003 African Flower
• High Boss™ embossing pad
• gold Class A Peels eyelets

Resist-Ink Tapestry (p36)
• Stamp: Stampendous ZE170 Mini Moth • Vivid™ multicoloured dye-based ink pad: Dynamic

Fading Flowers (p38)
• Stamp: Magenta G0301
• Marvy brush markers: purple, lime green, yellow, orange and turquoise

3-D Red Nosed Rudolph (p42)
• Stamp: Stamp Passions D4053 Ralph Reindeer

Chalk Checks (p44)
• Stamp: Hero Arts C2357 Straw Flower Sunburst • Stencils: Stampendous ET045 Stripes and Dots; Printworks Stripes and Dots

Translucent Dragonfly (p46)
• Stamp: Stampourri Inc S78 Dragonfly

Creative Craft Combo (p50)
• Stamps: Penny Black 2396E Daisy Border; Penny Black 2041E Flower Border

Gold Embossed Pansy (p52)
• Stamp: Penny Black 2408K Framed Pansy • Penny Black scroll card

Embossed Love Letter (p54)
• Stamp: PSX K3239
• Pearlustre™ embossing powder: rose quartz, amethyst, pearlized ruby and champagne pearl

Double Embossed Daisies (p56)
• Stamp: Stamp Studio Le Fleurs Tsukineko™ dual embossing pens: 53 garnet, 7 pansy, 34 lilac, 6 peony purple

Gold-on-Suede Poinsettia (p58)
• Stamp: PSX G3341 Poinsettia

Multi-Metallic Angel (p60)
• Stamp: Stampendous PO97 Angelica

Polymer Clay Peace Dove (p62)
• Stamps: Dove Stamp by Arthur Baker c/o ArtSeeds; Hero Arts C2523 Eternal

Scenic Art (p64)
• Stamps: Stamp Studio Flying Mallard; Stampendous N119 Winter Trees

Antique Heirloom Collage (p66)
• Stamps: Stampington Bashford Girls S7106; Leafy Notions S7100; Notions 4 57114; Stampman Shipping Script K16

Snowflake Windows (page 68)
• Stamp: Stampendous D106 Small Wire Snowflake

Mounting Magic (p70)
• Magenta soft floral background paper • Stamps: Magenta N/0293; Magenta N/0294

Shrink Plastic Heart (p74)
• Magenta Maruyama paper
• Stamp: Stampendous W041 Sketched Hearts

Christmas Tree Cutout (p76)
• Craft Work Cards Christmas Tree card • Stamps: Stampendous GO45 Star Border; PSX – F3339 Fir Trees; Stampendous H146 Wired Holly Ball; Stampendous M122 Snow Swirl • Permanent black Micron™ pen

Rose Series (p78)
• Stamp: Stampendous Maggie's Flower Set

Artful Embellishments (p80)
Woolly Sheep Tag
• Stamps: Rubber Stampede 735C Jumping Sheep; Stamp Studio Three Daisy Cluster
Glittered and Gilded Pine
• Stamp: Stampendous Y013 Ponderosa Pine
Wire-Haired Ballerina
• Stamp: Penny Black 2158H
Pearlized Wedding Attire
• Stamp: Stampendous R102 At The Altar

Suppliers

The author would like to thank the following suppliers for providing copyrighted images and/or products to enable her to produce this book.

UK

Craftwork Cards
Unit 7, The Moorings, Waterside Road, Stourton, Leeds
West Yorkshire LS10 1DG
tel: 0113 276 5713
fax: 01132 705986
email: Sue@craftworkcards. freeserve.co.uk
www.craftworkcards.com

The Stamp Man
8a Craven Court
High Street, Skipton
North Yorkshire BD23 1DG
tel/fax: 01756 797048
email: TheStampManUK@aol.com
www.thestampman.co.uk

Woodware BV
Unit 2a, Sandylands Business Park, Skipton, North Yorkshire BD23 2DE
tel: 01756 700024 .
fax: 01756 701097
email: sales@woodware.co.uk

USA

American Art Stamp
3870 Del Amo Boulevard
Torrance, CA 90503
tel: 310-371-6593
fax: 310-371-5545
email: AmArtStamp@aol.com
www.americanartstamp.com

Arthur Baker c/o ArtSeeds
PO Box 37041, Tucson, AZ 85740
tel: 520-219-0407
fax: 520 219-0559
email: Vakosmon@aol.com
www.artseeds.com

Artistic Wire Ltd
1210 Harrison Avenue
La Grange Park, IL 60526
tel: 630-530-7567
fax: 630-530-7536
email: Artwire97@aol.com
www.artisticwire.com

Clearsnap Inc
P O Box 98
Anacortes, WA 98221
tel: 360-293-6634
email: April.Thomas@ clearsnapinc.com
www.clearsnap.com

Emagination Crafts Inc
463 W Wrightwood Avenue
Elmhurst, IL 60126
tel: 630-833-9521
fax: 630-833-9751
email: service@ emaginationcrafts.com
www.emaginationcrafts.com

Hero Arts Rubber Stamps Inc
1343 Powell Street
Emeryville, CA 94608
tel: 800-822-HERO
fax: 800-441-3632
email: info@heroarts.com
www.heroarts.com

Making Tracks
P O Box 2045
Bigfork, MT 59911
tel: 406-755-6211
fax: 406-755-6262
email: greg@makingtracksink.com
www.makingtracksink.com

McGill Inc
131 East Praire Street
Marengo, IL 60152
tel: 815-568-7244
email: sales@mcgillinc.com
www.mcgillinc.com

Penny Black Rubber Stamps Inc
PO Box 11496, Berkeley, CA 94712
tel: 510-849-1883
fax: 510-849-1887
email: sales@pennyblackinc.com
www.pennyblackinc.com

PSX
360 Sutton Place
Santa Rosa, CA 95407
tel: 707-588-8058
fax: 707-588-7476
email: info@psxdesign.com
www.psxdesign.com

Ranger Industries Inc
15 Park Road
Tinton Falls, NJ 07724
tel: 732-389-3535
fax: 732-389-1102
www.rangerink.com

Rubber Stampede Inc
2550 Pellissier Place
Whittier, CA 90601
tel: 562-695-7969
email: advisor@dtccorp.com
www.rubberstampede.com

Stamp Studio Inc
1530 E Commercial Avenue,
Suite 109, Meridian, ID 83642
tel: 208-288-0300
fax: 208-895-0085
www.stampstudioinc.com

Stampa Rosa Inc
60 Maxwell Court
Santa Rosa, CA 95401

Stampendous Inc
1240 North Red Gum
Anaheim, CA 92806
tel: 714-688-0288
fax: 714-688-0297
email: stamp@stampendous.com
www.stampendous.com

Stampington & Company
22992 Mill Creek, Suite B
Laguna Hills, CA 92653
tel: 949-380-7318
fax: 949-380-9355
email: retail@stampington.com
www.stampington.com

Stampourri Inc
5952 Noonday Road
Hallsville, TX 75650
tel: 903-660-2420
fax: 903-660-2400
email: stampourri@aol.com
www.stampourri.com

Stewart Superior Corp
2050 Farallon Drive
San Leandro, CA 94577
tel: 510-346-9811
fax: 510-346-9822
email: sales@stewartsuperior.com
www.stewartsuperior.com

Terry Medaris Art Stamps
2211 N Camino Castile No 1218
Tucson, AZ 85715
tel: 520-296-4906
email: Medarisart@aol.com
www.terrymedarisartstamps.com

Tsukineko Inc
17640 NE 65th Street
Redmond, WA 98052
tel: 425-883-7733
fax: 425-883-7418
email: sales@tsukineko.com
www.tsukineko.com

Uchida of America Corp
3535 Del Amo Boulevard
Torrance, CA 90503
tel: 310-793-2200
fax: 800-229-7017
email: Marvy@Uchida.com
www.uchida.com

USArtQuest Inc
7800 Ann Arbor Road
Grass Lake, MI 49240
tel: 517-522-6225
fax: 517-522-6228
email: askanything@usartquest.com
www.usartquest.com

Canada
Magenta Rubber Stamps
2275 Bombardier Street
Sainte-Julie, Quebec J3H 3B4
tel: 450-922-5253
fax: 450-922-0053
email: info@Magentastyle.com
www.magentarubberstamps.com

Retailers
UK
Card Inspirations
The Old Dairy, Tewin Hill Farm
Tewin, Welwyn, Herts AL6 0LL
tel: 01438 717000
fax: 01438 717477
email: info@cardinspirations.biz
www.cardinspirations.co.uk

Centagraph
18 Station Parade, Harrogate
North Yorkshire HG1 1UE
tel: 01423 566327
fax: 01423 505486
email: info@centagraph.co.uk
www.centagraph.co.uk

The Craft Barn
9 East Grinstead Road
Lingfield, Surrey RH7 6EP
tel: 01342-832977
fax: 01342 836716
email: info@craftbarn.co.uk
www.craftbarn.co.uk

Craftwork Cards
(see Suppliers for details)

Dorrie Doodle
50 Bridge Street,
Aberdeen, AB11 6JN
tel/fax: 01224 212821
email: dorrie@dorriedoodle.com
www.dorriedoodle.com

Eclipse Cards and Crafts
Market Hall, Balcony Shop 4
Tennant Street, Derby DE1 2DB
tel: 01332 208308
fax: 08700 519195
email: info@eclipsecardcraft.co.uk
www.eclipsecardcraft.co.uk

LA Designs
26 High Street, Milford on Sea
Lymington, Hants SO41 0QF
tel/fax: 01590 644445
email: Lyn@LA-Designs.co.uk
www.LA-Designs.co.uk

The Stamp Man
(see Suppliers for details)

USA
Arnie's Arts & Crafts
3741 W Houghton Lane Drive
Houghton Lake, MI 48629
tel: 1-800-563-2356
email: info@arnies.com
www.arnies.com

Cracker Jack Gift Co
2 E State Street
Redlands, CA 92373
tel: 909-793-2200
www.crackerjackgifts.com

Kornely's Craft & Hobby Center
130 Front Street, PO Box 176
Beaver Dam, WI 53916
tel: 1-888-875-2768
email: barb@kornelys.com
www.kornelys.com

Stamp Diego
2650 Jamacha Road, Ste-139
El Cajon, CA 92019
tel: 1-800-845-2312
email: stampdiego@aol.com
www.stampdiego.com

Stamp Thyme
201 S State Street
Lockport, IL 60441
tel: 1-800-782-6793
email: stamp93@aol.com
www.stampthyme.com

Unique Impressions
1335 W Hwy 76
Branson, MO 65616
tel: 417-335-4817
email: uistamps@aol.com

Acknowledgments

A special thanks to the team that has worked on my book, especially Fiona, commissioning editor; Ali, executive art editor; Jennifer, desk editor; Jo, text editor; and Stewart and Ginette, photographers, for their unending patience and support.

To the artists who have taken time to share their artistic talents and creativity by contributing to projects and gallery cards, my grateful thanks: Fran Seiford, Vesta Abel, Hélène Métivier, Terry Medaris, Françoise Read, Maureen Blackman, Jill Tuck, Kim Reygate, Caroline Childs, Robin Bean, Sandra Williams, Jamie Martin and Jane Gill.

About the Author

Maggie Wright has many talents – she has studied interior design, floristry and Cordon Bleu cookery, and worked in the airline industry for many years. When her flying days were over, she started a small floristry business, and it was during a buying trip to Los Angeles for accessories that she came across the craft of rubber stamping. Seeing great potential in this art form, Maggie started and ran her own craft business for 12 years. The business was sold in 2002, and she is now a consultant to the rubber stamping industry. This is Maggie's third rubber stamping book, but her first for David & Charles. In addition to writing books, she contributes articles to *Crafts Beautiful* magazine, and has also been appointed the editor of rubber stamping magazine, *Stamping Art*.

Maggie lives in East Grinstead, West Sussex, England, and is kept busy with a family of four.

Index